Setting the World

on Fire

THE BRIEF, ASTONISHING LIFE of ST. CATHERINE of SIENA

SHELLEY EMLING

St. Martin's Press
New York

www.stmartins.com

Design by Letra Libre, Inc.

Library of Congress Cataloging-in-Publication Data

Names: Emling, Shelley.

Title: Setting the world on fire : the brief, astonishing life of St. Catherine of Siena / Shelley Emling.

Description: New York City : St. Martin's Press, 2016. | Includes index.

Identifiers: LCCN 2015033952 | ISBN 9781137279804 (hardback) | ISBN 9781466879195 (e-book)

Subjects: LCSH: Catherine, of Siena, Saint, 1347–1380. | Christian women saints—Italy—Siena—Biography. | Christian saints—Italy—Siena—Biography. | Women—Italy—Siena—Biography. | Siena (Italy)—Biography. | Siena (Italy)—History—1355–1557. | BISAC: BIOGRAPHY & AUTOBIOGRAPHY / Religious. | RELIGION / Christianity / Saints & Sainthood.

Classification: LCC BX4700.C4 E45 2016 | DDC 282.092—dc23

LC record available at http://lccn.loc.gov/2015033952

Our books may be purchased in bulk for promotional, educational, or business use. Please contact your local bookseller or the Macmillan Corporate and Premium Sales Department at 1-800-221-7945, extension 5442, or by e-mail at MacmillanSpecialMarkets@macmillan.com.

First Edition: April 2016

10 9 8 7 6 5 4 3 2 1

*To Ben and Olivia, both smart, sweet, savvy
and two of the four great loves of my life.*

*This book is also dedicated to girls and women
everywhere who, like Catherine of Siena, are
breaking the highest and hardest glass ceilings.*

Contents

Chronology   vii

Preface: An Astonishing Life   ix

Acknowledgments   xix

One   A Bright Little Girl   I

Two   A First Glimpse of Christ   19

Three   Kiss Me with a Kiss of Your Mouth   35

Four   Just What the Times Needed   53

Five   Fighting Off Threats   71

Six   Bearing the Wounds of Christ   89

Seven   The Spilling of Blood   105

Eight   The Move to Rome   121

Nine   Brilliant Work   139

Ten   A Turn for the Worse   157

Eleven   Spiritual Anxieties   175

Twelve   The End of a Saintly Existence   193

Epilogue   A Woman's Legacy   209

Selected Bibliography   219

Index   221

Eight pages of illustrations appear between pages 104 and 105.

Chronology

1226	Saint Francis of Assisi, the other patron saint of Italy, dies.
1309	The pope moves from Rome to Avignon, France.
1337	The Hundred Years' War between France and England begins.
1347	Catherine is born in Siena on March 25.
1348	The plague decimates Siena and much of Europe.
1353–54	Catherine sees her first vision of Christ.
1364	Catherine becomes a member of the Mantellate.
1366–67	Catherine has "mystical marriage" with Jesus.
1370	Catherine experiences a "mystical death."
1375	Catherine receives the stigmata in Pisa.
1377–78	The pope returns to Rome.
1378	Catherine goes to Florence on a peacekeeping mission.
1380	Catherine dies in Rome on April 29.
1461	Catherine is canonized.
1939	Catherine becomes patron saint of Italy, along with Francis of Assisi.
1970	Catherine is declared a Doctor of the Church.

PREFACE

An Astonishing Life

It is not the hour to seek one's self for one's self, nor to flee pains in order to possess consolations; nay, it is the hour to lose one's self.

—Catherine of Siena

For the Italians, food has always been one of life's greatest pleasures. Whether it's pork or lamb, olives or grapes, the sun-soaked peninsula has it, and it's good. Yet when Italy, one of the world's great centers of gastronomy, settled on a patron saint, it chose someone who did everything she could to avoid eating. And it ended up killing her.

That saint was Catherine Benincasa, the frolicsome, imaginative twenty-fourth child of a kind and somewhat prosperous wool dyer. Catherine was born in Siena, a town of economic and political prominence very near Florence, on March 25, 1347, the Feast of the Annunciation—a day when people celebrate the angel Gabriel's appearance to the Virgin Mary by devouring angel food cake and other baked goods. Perched atop three hills and one of the best-preserved medieval cities in Italy, Siena today looks much as it did in the Middle Ages. The town's sloping, shell-shaped Piazza del Campo—still one of the most spectacular open urban spaces in Europe—was newly paved with brick and stone the year before Catherine's birth. Even as a little girl, Catherine had such a strong sense of self that, at the tender age of seven, she promised her virginity to Christ. Later she had another vision in which Jesus declared his intention to make her his bride. The ring? Christ's foreskin, traditionally removed at circumcision. As a teenager, Catherine chopped off her hair in a sign of defiance against being overly groomed by her mother to attract a husband. In her 20s, she received the stigmata, or the spontaneous display on her body of the same wounds Christ received when crucified. As a young woman, her public influence soared because of her reputation for holiness and wisdom. The unschooled mystic commanded popes and kings—as well as ordinary people—to do the will of God. With the artfulness of Botticelli, this daughter of a merchant mixed mysticism and practical ministry, and was never once intimidated by powerful men.

Although she was illiterate, her major theological treatise on the whole of mankind's spiritual life, *The Dialogue,* as well as 385 letters and 26 prayers—all dictated to secretaries—are considered among the most brilliant works of early church literature. They are filled with emotive rhetoric about being washed in the blood of Jesus; in fact, it's possible that no one in church history has been as enamored with blood as Catherine. In 2010, Pope Benedict XVI described these writings as "a masterpiece" that still speaks to Christians today. In 2008, a comprehensive English translation of the saint's letters was published as a four-volume series thanks to the work of Sister Suzanne Noffke, an internationally renowned Catherinian scholar. In addition to Catherine's own writings, a detailed biography by Raymond of Capua, Catherine's most important spiritual adviser and very dear friend, is a vital source for what we know about Catherine today.

While Catherine may have grown up in an average medieval family, with parents and siblings who not only provided for her but who also downright doted on her, the adult Catherine spurned their earthly needs for food and drink with a passion that bordered on the psychotic. In the Middle Ages, control over one's body was seen as a way of achieving oneness with God. As a result, many revered religious women in the history of the Catholic Church cultivated a love-hate relationship with eating. Another Catherine from Italy, St. Catherine of Genoa, followed in Catherine of Siena's footsteps, as did many others, about a century later. This Catherine also ate very little and wouldn't take in so much as a bite during Lent and the 40 days preceding Christmas. But Catherine of Siena took patterns of self-starvation to legendary extremes. She shoved sticks down her throat to make herself vomit. She sipped the pus of the sick and longed to quench her thirst with blood.

Catherine's aversion to food started early. Galvanized by her faith, she attempted her first fast when she was only six or seven years old, just after Jesus came to her in a vision, the first of many that would power her extraordinary life. By the time she reached 12 or 13—the point at which most girls of that era were married off—Catherine refused to eat meat and hot food or to drink wine and subsisted for the most part on morsels of bread and herbs, sips of cold water, and the Eucharist, which she lusted after constantly. The paltry diet caused her to stop menstruating shortly after going through puberty—when she was barely into her teens. Sleep, too, proved elusive; she rarely napped more than an hour or two a night. Early on, she also made a habit of flogging herself three times a day: once for her own sins, once for the sins of others still alive, and once for the sins of those who had died. After years of such deprivations, this woman with such an appetite for self-mortification reached a point where she could no longer digest even a single bite of food without suffering serious pain. Curiously, she had absolutely no problem whatsoever encouraging others to partake of that which she disdained, distributing copious amounts of food and wine to those in need. Just as Jesus was said to have fed 5,000 people with only five loaves of bread and two fish—the only miracle that's recorded in all four Gospels—Catherine managed to miraculously multiply bread and wine to satisfy the hungry during times of scarcity, as was corroborated by several of her contemporaries.

She actually seemed to derive energy not from taking food in but from the act of giving it away.

But not everyone was blindly enthralled by Catherine and her devoutness. Even in the 1300s, a time when faith was woven into every aspect of daily life, there were skeptics who claimed she must be either eating in secret or relying on some kind of demonic intervention. But by many reliable accounts, she consumed nothing but daily Holy Communion in her final years. At times, she so craved the Eucharist that her heart raced and her teeth chattered audibly in suspense. Once she took it, she would either writhe in ecstasy or lie on the floor, stiff as a board, for three or four hours at a time, sometimes speaking plainly and loudly, sometimes uttering nothing but gibberish. Cynics often questioned these spiritual raptures, physically poking and kicking her in an effort to see whether it was all just an act.

More than 600 years later, this paradigmatic personality still strikes us as astonishing. Her life was a tireless campaign against arrogance, corruption and selfishness. More than a century before Martin Luther penned his 1517 document attacking corruption in the Catholic Church, Catherine recognized that the institution was at a crossroads and that the old ways of thinking would no longer suffice. She called out even the highest ranks of the clergy for their avarice and bloated pride. She wore herself out seeking creative new solutions to conflicts. She convinced the pope to leave Avignon, France, and return to Rome after a nearly 70-year absence. She was arguably as pious as Francis of Assisi—so significant that the current pope, Pope Francis, chose to take his name—but not nearly as well known.

Indeed, Catherine is a theological giant, equal in stature to the likes of St. Thomas Aquinas, also a great believer in the idea that, through free will, people have the power to shape their own lives. The two are conceivably among the most important theologians and are central figures in the history of Roman Catholicism, Western civilization's decisive spiritual force for nearly 2,000 years. There are more than a billion Catholics on the planet—16 percent of the world's population—spread out across six continents. What binds them together is not only their belief in Jesus Christ and their obedience to the papacy—the oldest continuing absolute monarchy in the world—but also their veneration of saints, whom they see as role models. Although the percentage of Catholics who consider themselves "strong" members of the church was at an all-time low in 2012, the phenomenal personal popularity of Pope Francis, elected in 2013, has helped reinvigorate this complex institution. In 2014, Pope Francis referred to Catherine during a general audience at the Vatican, encouraging the young to "learn from her how to live with the clear conscience of those who do not bend to human compromises."

Catherine's story, while on the surface a bit bizarre, is still germane to people today. As Father Alfredo White, an expert on St. Catherine at the San Domenico Basilica in Siena, put it in 2015, "We still believe saints are in heaven and that they know about our struggles and that they can help us. We can strive to imitate their virtues even 600 or 700 years later." Believers in Catherine's "mystical marriage" with Jesus and other miracles attached to her personal history would be run out of town by modern generations, but there is enough contemporaneous testimony detailing her implausible life—not to mention the translations of Catherine's own letters—to suggest an existence made extraordinary by wondrous moments. Catherine is not the only person in history who saw visions. Indeed, religious visionaries have been present in every faith and era, including our own. She was unique, though, in that she viewed her complete surrender to God as a goal to be reached through time, helped along by the encouragement of her visual encounters with Christ. Even Catherine's death at the age of 33 is worth noting. Throughout history, many people known as mystics died at 33. The number three, of course, refers to the Holy Trinity—the Father, Son and Holy Spirit. The traditional belief is that Jesus, too, died at 33.

No book on the life of Catherine would be complete without an examination of the Dominicans, the Catholic religious order founded in 1214 by St. Dominic de Guzman, a Spanish priest. Not wanting to be trapped in a convent, Catherine joined a group of supportive Dominican laywomen in her town—mostly older widows—when only a teenager. Although the monastic life is generally associated with solemnity, jubilance is actually one of the great hallmarks of Dominican life. Blaise Pascal, the French philosopher, was once overheard to remark, "Nobody is as happy as a real Christian." For many of history's greatest preachers—including Catherine—the attainment of happiness was not a matter of chance, but rather the result of an intentional seeking of happiness for others. And yet selflessness never excluded a sense of fun. Even St. Thomas Aquinas took to task those so serious they failed to have a sense of humor. People lacking in merriment, he wrote, are morally unsound. Suspicious even. Certainly in the Dominican tradition there is no shame in laughter—even raucous, uncontrollable laughter. Catherine herself enjoyed a teasing sense of humor.

One of the things I like most about Catherine is how she was able to get what she wanted by being forthright but never rude. By adroitly blending boldness with humility, she persuaded Pope Gregory XI to return the papacy from France to Rome—an action that galvanizes feminists even today—but she never once doubted his authority, not for a second. Instead, she told him, "*Esto vir!*" You are the man. You are the boss. Use your position of power. She also stressed in her writings to politicians and nobility that a ruler can't be effective unless he, first and foremost, walks in integrity. "Politics are never anything but the product of a person's religious life," she wrote. "Break the chains of sin; cleanse yourself by confession. Only then will you be real rulers. For who can really be master if he is not master of himself, if reason does not rule his passions?"

Catherine's world was one of tragedy, violence and corruption. During the fourteenth century, the Italian city-states battled against each other, and against the papacy, for power. The Hundred Years' War raged on, during which England tried and ultimately failed to take control of continental France. The church, too, was in turmoil, losing much of its spiritual edge during this time. In 1309, the pope moved his court from Rome to Avignon and remained there until 1377. The papacy also waged a war against Muslim forces in the Holy Land—a war that even the peace-loving Catherine rallied in favor of.

The end of the Middle Ages and the beginning of the Renaissance was a time of massive cultural, economic, political, religious and social change—with all the insecurity, confusion and upheaval that go along with it. In the twelfth century, the great reformer St. Bernard of Clairvaux compared the Catholic Church, infested at the time with vice and immorality, to a resurrected version of Sodom and Gomorrah. As a result, the Middle Ages also became a time of spiritual agony during which many people lost faith in the institution. A fractured Catholic Church struggled then, much as the modern Catholic Church has struggled in the last few decades. Catherine herself traveled widely to push for the internal reform of the church. She worked tirelessly to foster peace in a fractious Europe. She exhorted even the pope to greater holiness.

All of this contributed to a legacy as lasting as her life was short. Canonized by Pope Pius II in 1461, Catherine was the original breaker of glass ceilings. Her many feats earned her the distinction, along with St. Francis of Assisi, of being named the patron saint of Italy. It also earned her the title of Doctor of the Church, one of only four women to be so honored. Further, Pope John Paul II proclaimed her co-patroness of Europe in 1999, along with St. Bridget of Sweden and St. Teresa Benedicta of the Cross, also known as Edith Stein. John Paul said of Catherine's work: "The uninhibited, powerful and incisive tone in which she admonished priests, Bishops and Cardinals is quite striking."

Amid the relentless rise in narcissism in our culture, a look at someone who was completely and utterly selfless has been, for me, refreshing and motivating. Her words compel us to put others before ourselves and to attend to anyone suffering with as much care as possible. Her core message was that every Christian is called to live "in the blood," that is, in service to his or her neighbor.

A modern Catherine, Catherine Middleton, married Prince William on April 29, 2011, the Feast of St. Catherine of Siena and the date of her death. Following the couple's exchange of vows, the bishop of London read aloud the saint's most famous words: "Be who God meant you to be and you will set the world on fire."

St. Catherine of Siena was one woman who did just that.

Acknowledgments

When an editor first mentioned the idea of writing a book about St. Catherine of Siena, I was—initially—a bit hesitant. As a Presbyterian who grew up Lutheran, I had only vaguely heard of her. Sure, I had some Catholic friends, but the only saint I recalled them ever mentioning was St. Anthony—and then only when they were looking for something. I decided to think about it. The very next day I was driving near my home in Montclair, New Jersey, and for whatever reason, I got turned around trying to find our vet's office. Frustrated, I pulled into a parking lot. When I looked up, I did a double take. The huge sign in front of me said "Saint Catherine of Siena School." I had driven through this adjacent Cedar Grove, New Jersey, neighborhood a thousand times but had never noticed this place before.

True story. And so I began looking into St. Catherine's place in history—and I'm incredibly glad I did.

Yet, to say it's difficult to write about someone who lived seven centuries ago is a gross understatement. It simply can't be done without the help of those who have gone before. I am indebted to many writers, but most especially Raymond of Capua, whose *Life of Catherine of Siena*, completed in 1395, is a valuable resource, even if it was written mostly to make a case for sainthood. I'm also grateful to other extremely talented writers and translators, including Sigrid Undset, Thomas McDermott, Edmund G. Gardner, Don Brophy, Barbara W. Tuchman, F. Thomas Luongo, David Winner, Frances Stonor Saunders, Elizabeth A. Dreyer, Caroline Walker Bynum, Jane Tylus, Ted Harrison, Mary Catherine Hilkert, Suzanne Noffke, David H. Lukenbill, Rudolph M. Bell and John Kelly.

I also want to thank Mary Catherine Hilkert, O.P., Dr. Gemma Simmonds, Professor Karen Scott, Professor Elizabeth Petroff and Father Alfredo White in Siena for their time.

Personally, I must thank the tireless Agnes Birnbaum, the most attentive literary agent in the world. Our lunches together are such a treat. Also, I've had many editors in my career, but none as conscientious and encouraging as Elisabeth Dyssegaard, executive editor at St. Martin's Press. Also thanks to Laura Apperson and others at St. Martin's for their hard work on my behalf.

I've drawn a great deal of inspiration from my many thoughtful Catholic friends, especially Mary Messier. I'm grateful to all of you. Thanks to everyone on my block—especially Christine and Norm James, who are such generous friends and cheerleaders. Thanks to my girlfriends—especially you lovely ladies in London, Texas and New Jersey—who all bring me immeasurable joy. Thanks to my aunt Karen, my mother-in-law Ginger and my sister Paula for always being so interested in everything I'm doing.

Not a day goes by that I'm not grateful to my crazy-smart husband, Scott, for reading every chapter and for putting up with endless chitchat about the Catholic Church in the Middle Ages. A mountain of appreciation also goes to my three beautiful children, Chris, Ben and Olivia, who've been without a mom most weekends. Without you four, this would all mean very little. (Thanks to you, too, Pepper!)

As always, my loudest shout-out in the world goes to my mother, Lois Ruth, who showed me every day what being selfless really means. I continue to miss her every day of my life.

Finally, I drew so much inspiration from Catherine Benincasa herself, who had so many extraordinary qualities. But the quality I love most is her selflessness. She helped anyone and everyone regardless of how sick or poor they were, without ever giving a thought to her own needs. She fought against pride and aimed for perfect humility. What a breath of fresh air for those of us living in the "me, me, me" twenty-first century. My hope is that you will allow her to inspire you as she did me.

ONE

A Bright Little Girl

For the residents of Tuscany, the year 1348 must have felt like the end of the world. Even from nearly 5,000 miles away, by way of merchants traveling along the ancient international passageway known as the Silk Road, the Italians heard rumblings of something sinister percolating in central Asia that would soon test the faith of even the most faithful like nothing ever had before. The fourteenth-century plague—or the Black Death, as it would later be called— wiped out nearly one-third of the people of China before the rest of the world knew what was coming. Tracking very precisely the medieval trade routes across the Black Sea and into the Mediterranean that brought European customers silk, porcelain and other goods, the plague first descended on Europe in 1345–1346 with the Mongol attack on the city of Kaffa, a bustling seaport on the Crimean Peninsula. During the siege, some members of the Mongol army became infected with the plague. When comrades died, the Mongols lobbed the bodies over the city's walls, an early version of biological warfare. Some infected sailors—covered in mysterious black boils—managed to flee in Genoese trading ships bound for Italy. When the ships docked at the port of Messina on the island of Sicily in October 1347, citizens were aghast at all the dying sailors who were aboard. Acting fast, the Italians banished the ships back out to sea—but it was too late. At least some of the very ill, as one chronicler put it, had already tumbled out of the galleys "with sickness clinging to their very bones." One of the greatest scourges of all time had arrived.

Europe was a perfect breeding ground for the disease. Densely populated cities—the number of European inhabitants shot up from 38 million to 74 million in the three centuries leading up to 1300—only accelerated its circulation. Unsanitary conditions pervaded the medieval continent with many streets nothing more than meandering cesspools of fetid water. Butchers slaughtered animals outdoors, leaving the unusable scraps for dogs and cats to fight over. Bathrooms were a curious luxury. Most people used chamber pots that were emptied into open sewers, which usually fed into nearby rivers and creeks. Lice and bugs played no favorites, swarming in the homes of both the rich and the poor. The stench of cities was so bad that some people held scented handkerchiefs to their noses to keep from vomiting.

After striking Sicily in 1347, the plague followed a circular path through Europe. Droves of people across Italy, France, England, Germany, eastern Europe and even Russia collapsed like dominoes before the disease finally exhausted itself in 1351. In London alone, nearly half the population—perhaps 40,000 people—perished during the 18 months between the fall of 1348 and the spring of 1350. Medical knowledge was sorely lacking, and people knew nothing about contagious diseases. The only thing people knew with 100 percent certainty was that a harrowing sequence of symptoms came on swiftly, followed by certain death 24 to 48 hours later. The first sign was sneezing (hence the origin of the phrase "God bless you," a protective charm designed to save the sneezer from evil). And they knew there was no cure.

The epidemic was so rampant and spread so fast that dazed family members had no choice but to walk out on each other as soon as any one of them exhibited even a hint of fever, chills, headache or weakness. Lawyers refused to draw up wills for the infected. Doctors refused to see patients. Parents shunned their own children; children shunned their parents. Shop owners closed stores. Existing societal and economic structures came unraveled faster than you could say "Pope Clement." As a result, multitudes of the sick were abandoned without any care. With towns reporting hundreds of deaths every day, people perished without the benefit of last rites or the confession of sins, a prospect that must have horrified medieval Christians who didn't want to risk missing out on heaven. So scarce were priests, themselves wiped out in great numbers, that people were allowed to make confessions to laymen or, in a worst-case scenario, to women. With bloated bodies piling up in the streets, Pope Clement VI had no choice but to consecrate the entire Rhône River, which instantly transformed it into a holy place to lay the dead. Soon a perpetual stream of corpses drifted slowly into the Mediterranean Sea. Those bodies lucky enough to be buried in the ground—often by desperate members of the lowest class who were paid sky-high wages—were stacked on top of each other, separated by thin layers of clay, "just as one makes lasagna with layers of pasta and cheese," in the words of one chronicler.

In a century in which nothing traveled faster than the speediest horse, the extent of the plague's contagious power couldn't have been more jarring. Whole families were wiped out in one fell swoop. In enclosed communities such as prisons, convents and monasteries, the infection of one generally spelled the demise of the entire institution. One observer wrote about plague victims eating lunch with their friends and "dinner with their ancestors in paradise." It's no wonder then that, at least for a few somber years, millions of people began to seriously contemplate the end of civilization and, with it, the extinction of the human race.

The chaos gave rise to various bizarre movements, including a group of Christian men known as the Brotherhood of the Flagellants, which flourished despite the church's considerable efforts to tamp it down. These zealots believed the disease was God's retribution against a sinful world that had long ago lost its moral footing. In their desire to appease him, the Flagellants marched barefoot throughout Europe's biggest cities, beating their backs and shoulders with weighted scourges until blood soaked through their white robes and dripped down their legs. Anyone unfortunate enough to witness this public manifestation of self-sacrifice was horrified. The Flagellants were extremely anti-Semitic—but they were far from the only ones. Outbursts of hateful anti-Semitism were common even before the disease, and the apocryphal nature of the plague sparked even more virulent attacks against Jews—already isolated outsiders. To some, the only plausible explanation for death on so massive a scale was human wickedness. Surely, they contended, someone must be behind the spread of the plague, perhaps by poisoning the wells, and who better to blame than vindictive Jews dead-set on killing Christians and dominating the world? Everyone seemed to overlook the fact that the death toll held steady for all segments of the population—Jews included. Panic reigned supreme, and everybody was looking for a scapegoat.

The Italian writer Giovanni Boccaccio lived through the epidemic and gave a chilling description of the toll the disease took:

The symptoms were not the same as in the East, where a gush of blood from the nose was the plain sign of inevitable death; but it began both in men and women with certain swellings in the groin or under the armpit. They grew to the size of a small apple or an egg, more or less, and were vulgarly called tumors. In a short space of time, these tumors spread from the two parts named all over the body. Soon after this the symptoms changed and black or purple spots appeared on the arms or thighs or any other part of the body, sometimes a few large ones, sometimes many little ones. These spots were a certain sign of death, just as the original tumor had been and still remained.

No doctor's advice, no medicine could overcome or alleviate this disease. An enormous number of ignorant men and women set up as doctors in addition to those who were trained. Either the disease was such that no treatment was possible or the doctors were so ignorant that they did not know what caused it, and consequently could not administer the proper remedy. In any case very few recovered; most people died within about three days of the appearance of the tumors described above.

The plague's greatest blow to the medieval Christian way of thinking, he noted, was the idea of being buried far away from one's own church and family.

"Such was the multitude of corpses brought to the churches every day and almost every hour that there was not enough consecrated ground to give them burial, especially since they wanted to bury each person in the family grave, according to old custom. Although the cemeteries were full they were forced to dig huge trenches, where they buried the bodies by hundreds. Here they stowed them away like bales in the hold of a ship and covered them with a little earth, until the whole trench was full."

By 1353, the pandemic had carried off anywhere from 25 percent to 60 percent of Europe's population. The Black Death was originally thought to be an epidemic of the bubonic plague, caused by the bacterium *Yersinia pestis* and contracted from infected fleas living on rats. However, scientists from Public Health England in 2014 drew a stunning new conclusion: the disease that decimated Europe in 1348 moved so quickly that it must also have been airborne, spread from person to person through coughing, sneezing or breathing. In other words, the plague actually may have been pneumonic—not bubonic.

Airborne or not, the plague turned life into a grim, grisly battle for the people of Tuscany. As one might expect, the elderly and the very young were especially likely to succumb to infection, with newborn children the most vulnerable. Some 50 to 60 percent of all Tuscans perished. In Siena alone, the population plummeted from 42,000 before the plague to around 14,000 by 1350. But as indiscriminate as the Black Death was, the disease somehow managed to skip over at least a few very fortunate households— including one in Siena headed by a kindhearted wool dyer and his spirited wife—almost as if by divine providence.

Somehow the God-fearing dyer Giacomo di Benincasa and his outspoken bride, Lapa di Puccio di Piagente, the daughter of a businessman and a poet of some renown, survived the catastrophe mostly unscathed. They lived and worked in a fairly spacious three-story house—one that still stands today—in which Giacomo's workshop was also located on the bottom floor. Built against the side of a hill on Via dei Tintori, or the Street of Dyers, the home was close to the Fontebranda, the oldest and most impressive of the fountains supplying fresh water to the town. Sitting in the shadow of the Basilica of San Domenico, the fountain had been rebuilt, entirely in brick, in 1246. The couple needed a house with lots of space—even the family name means "well-housed"—as they were raising a large brood of active boys and girls. By the time Catherine and her twin sister, Giovanna, came along, born in a second-floor bedroom on March 25, 1347, Lapa, then age 40, already had given birth to 22 other children, a massive number by today's standards and considered unusually large even in the 1300s. The date of Catherine's birth was an auspicious one as it not only marked the beginning of the new year but was also the day the Catholic Church celebrated the Feast of the Annunciation. Indeed, before the advent of the Gregorian calendar in 1582, March 25 was celebrated as the day of Christ's conception, nine months before his birth on December 25. Catherine's birth also came 120 years after the death of St. Francis of Assisi—often described as Catherine's brother in spirit—in the arms of Lady Poverty, which is how he described his life of extreme austerity.

Lapa could nurse only one of her new twins, so sickly little Giovanna was placed in the care of a wet nurse, while the charmed Catherine was weaned on her mother's milk. Since so many pregnancies had forced Lapa to hand her babies off to other women, Catherine became the first infant Lapa had been able to successfully breastfeed. Years later, Lapa would concede that Catherine had been her favorite child. Giovanna died in infancy, and Lapa went on to have one more baby, a girl named Giovanna in memory of Catherine's twin. But she died when Catherine was 16, in 1363. In general, though, Giocomo and Lapa were fortunate to have the chance to bring up even one-third of their children at a time when the infant mortality rate was exceptionally high.

In Siena, Giacomo was known for being kind, smart, honest and markedly mild-mannered—so much so that he sometimes annoyed his vociferous wife. Once, when he refused to make extortion payments demanded of him by a conniving competitor, Giacomo opted to suffer slander rather than utter even one bad word against the man. When Lapa denounced the person to her husband, Giacomo replied, "Leave him be in peace. You will see that God will show him his fault and protect us." And, as Lapa later revealed, that's exactly what happened. The man apologized and cleared the family's good name. This kind of generous, soft-hearted demeanor helped Giacomo become a well-liked and somewhat prominent businessman and a full member of the cliquish wool guild, an affinity that was no trivial matter. As a member, he was allowed to vote in state elections and hold public office. During these years, the export trade was inextricably linked with wool, and dyeing was an important cog in the wheel of a prosperous local economy. Indeed, wool was the most popular material for clothing, mostly because it could hold dye so well. No doubt the importance of wool was one of the reasons friends and family held Giacomo in such high esteem. Lapa, too, was revered, coming from an established merchant family. From what we know, Giacomo and Lapa made a good team. Whereas she was impulsive and loud—and lived to be nearly 100—he was practical and calm and died when he was middle-aged.

Of Catherine's siblings, her brother Bartolomeo made the most fortuitous union by marrying Lisa Colombini, the pious niece of Giovanni Colombini, one of the most fascinating characters ever to come out of Siena. In midlife, this wealthy merchant suddenly found God, becoming so deeply religious that he handed all his belongings over to charity so that he might live a life of abject poverty. Wearing little more than rags, he criss-crossed Tuscany, preaching against the evils of money. He tended the sick, donated to charity and turned his home into a refuge for the poor—all of which won him a loyal fan base. Catherine would go on to become very close to her sister-in-law Lisa as well as being one of Giovanni's biggest supporters.

The prosperous decades enjoyed by the Benincasa family leading up to Catherine's birth mirrored those of Siena, which boasted a pre-plague population of well over 40,000 in 1347. Northern and central Italy as a whole was flourishing, being on the trade route between the eastern Mediterranean and northern Europe. Siena—a heavily fortified hub in the heart of the Tuscan countryside 30 miles south of Florence—and the other cities of the region grew in wealth as they acquired more and more of the land surrounding them. Eventually these so-called city-states became in effect independent—and competitive. Indeed, these centers of population expended a substantial amount of energy trying to one-up each other, in both military and economic terms. Culturally, too, the Tuscan region played a decisive role in the birth of the Italian Renaissance some five decades later. Home to artists, writers and philosophers, including Dante Alighieri, Francesco Petrarch and Giovanni Boccaccio, the region helped revolutionize art and literature. When it came to language, the Tuscan dialect was the one that emerged dominant in Italy's political and cultural circles by the fourteenth century. Although Italian first showed up in written documents during the tenth century—usually in notes inserted into Latin documents—there was for a long time no standard written or spoken language in Italy. Therefore, writers had two options: they could write in Latin or in their own regional dialect. It was the dialect of the culturally important Florence that would become the basis of the modern Italian language. Incidentally, Catherine was the first woman to write in that powerful Florence vernacular, or the popular spoken language of the region.

To Siena's south was Rome, the first city in the world to exceed a population of one million. But by the fourteenth century, even it paled in comparison to the brightness of its northern neighbors. Although the city reigned supreme in Europe for more than 1,000 years, it was by the 1300s nothing but a shadow of its former self, with a crumbling infrastructure and its famed Colosseum and other once-beautiful monuments in various states of disrepair. In comparison with Rome, Siena and the other cities of northern and central Italy were on an upward trajectory toward unrivaled social, political and economic success. This entire region with its formidable wool industry and bankers who were known to be masters of international commerce was thriving. A new commercial class was flush with material goods—and optimism about the future. Accelerated immigration from the countryside infused the economy with much-needed laborers. So many residents of surrounding villages poured into Siena that the city was soon bursting at the seams. To at least some financial experts, this time—in this place—gave impetus to capitalist market ideology. Historians, too, often describe the Renaissance that began in the late 1300s as the start of modern history, for it was during this period that many of the traits of contemporary modern Western society took shape.

Buoyed by their good fortune, Tuscans developed an affinity for extravagance with a particular penchant for opulent churches, fountains and municipal buildings. In Siena, the pinnacle of civic pride came in 1339, nearly a decade before Catherine's birth, when church officials decided to expand their cathedral—built between 1215 and 1263—to such a degree that it would become the largest in Christendom, a church so grand it would dwarf even St. Peter's in Rome. The Sienese were also notoriously clean. The city imposed a ban on keeping pigs inside the city walls as well as one on throwing garbage into the streets. Every so often, a housewife might still have splashed the contents of garbage pails and washtubs out of a second-floor window, but she at least had the decency to shout *"Guarda!"*—or "look out below"—first.

And then, in what must have felt like an instant, everything changed.

The plague helped devastate the economy, and a cooler climate wreaked havoc on agricultural productivity. In order to finance the many wars of the century, the government was forced to raise taxes, crippling the finances of average families. Leaders tried revoking the ban on gambling that had been imposed in an effort to appease an angry God. But this did little to stuff the coffers. Without even a port to sustain it, Siena hobbled off the world stage—and stayed there for centuries. Progress on the expansion of the cathedral sputtered along and finally came to a complete stop. Prices skyrocketed; businesses flopped. Laborers—now in short supply—commanded such high wages that few cash-strapped employers could afford them. In the years leading up to 1348, people in Siena and Florence had been teeming with sanguinity, enjoying the most comfortable lives in the cities' histories. But almost overnight, any certainty of life—and even any hope of a good death—blew away like dust.

But the plague was not simply a tragedy with tangible repercussions. Following an initial frantic outpouring of piety, the magnitude of the calamity began chipping away little by little at the intangible faith people had in bedrock assumptions they'd blindly lived by for generations. Disillusioned with the new world order, people grew angry, worried and distrustful of institutions. They were panicked about what horror might strike next, certain God was out to get them. Some devolved into all manner of debauchery and promiscuity, choosing to worship at the altar of wicked pleasures. Others clung more tightly to their faith, convinced that God was trying to teach them a lesson. People looked to the church for some measure of comfort. But there wasn't any. The feelings of bitterness that resulted helped pave the way for Martin Luther's split from the Catholic Church and the emergence of Protestant-ism more than a century later. Yes, there were many accounts of nuns, friars and priests giving their lives to care for the infected during the plague. But there were also many accounts of clergy refusing to go anywhere near the sick, which left vulnerable flocks to fend for themselves. Making a bad situation even worse was the closing of so many churches due to the deaths of their priests. For some time, people had been craving better pastoral care and a greater emphasis on clerical morality. For them, the church's woe-ful behavior during the plague was the last straw.

For more than 400 years, the Catholic Church had held sway over every part of life in Europe, both religious and secular. Faith had been the stabilizing constant in everyday life that bound dis-parate communities together. No one questioned the authority of the pope. But by the 1300s, the church began losing much of its footing as a pillar of moral leadership, not only because of the plague, but also because of the illness festering inside its own walls. Ruling just before the plague era was one of history's most scandal-ridden pontiffs, Boniface VIII, who was said to have kept a married woman and her daughter as mistresses before his elec-tion. Even after he became pope in 1294, his sexual exploits went unabated. He was one of the most avid supporters of papal author-ity—in matters both spiritual and temporal—and his squabbles with King Philip IV of France over a government's ability to tax clergy members were legendary, erupting into an excommunica-tion of the king in 1303 and an issuance of the most famous papal document of the Middle Ages. In unequivocal terms, the decree stated that it was absolutely necessary for salvation that "every hu-man creature be subject to the Roman pontiff."

The enduring enmity between Boniface and Dante Alighieri is remembered even today. The great Italian writer got poetic justice by placing the pope in the Eighth Circle of Hell in his *Divine Comedy*, right alongside the simoniacs who were reviled for buying and selling ecclesiastical offices and pardons. After Boniface's death in 1303, Clement V, a Frenchman, was elected pope, and his first course of action was to appoint nine French cardinals. Since cardinals voted on who would be pope, these new additions ensured that the next ones were likely to be French. And they were. At the urging of King Philip IV, Clement decided in 1309 to pull up stakes and move his residence, his staff and the entire base of Catholicism to Avignon, a small city in southern France close to the Italian border. But the move didn't end hostilities. During the upcoming years, the popes in France found themselves increasingly under the thumb of the arrogant and somewhat neurotic King Philip, who often behaved as though the papacy was nothing but an extension of French foreign policy.

Once the papacy moved, churchmen abandoned almost all pretense of being upright and moral. Pope Clement VI, elected in 1342, set off a period of particularly extraordinary papal extravagance, with popes openly selling church offices and using bribery to obtain power. Most everything carried a price tag, including ecclesiastical offices, holy relics and pardons for sins. For a stipend, priests were even allowed by their bishops to have mistresses. Devoted to lavish living, Clement enlarged the papal palace and surrounded himself with artists, scholars and musicians. The moral disarray was so bad that St. Bridget of Sweden—typically a staunch supporter of the pope's authority—refused to visit Avignon. She publicly attacked the papacy as a field "full of pride, avarice, self-indulgence and corruption." So obscene were Clement's excesses that he was referred to as an unfit and drunken helmsman of the church by the poet Francesco Petrarch. But even Clement had his limits. One day he launched a tirade against his fellow churchmen: "What can you preach to the people? If on humility, you yourselves are the proudest of the world, puffed up, pompous and sumptuous in luxuries. If on poverty, you are so covetous that all the benefices of the world are not enough for you. If on chastity—but we will be silent on this, for God knows what each man does and how many of you satisfy your lusts."

Of course, not every pope of Avignon was inept and immoral. A few made great strides, one of which was to expand missionary efforts as far as China. But for the most part, the lavish lifestyles of supposedly humble churchmen wrought disgust. Even today, the majestic height of the fourteenth-century Palace of the Popes, rising high above every other building so that it can be seen from almost anywhere in Avignon, acts as a reminder of their folly. Beyond all the corruption, the so-called Avignon Captivity of the papacy—which lasted nearly 70 years—also chipped away at the prestige of the Catholic Church for another reason. Abandoning the "city of Peter" just didn't sit right with Christians. After all, the apostle—believed to have been given authority over the entire church by Christ—was thought to have founded the institution in Rome. He was later martyred and buried there.

The Avignon Captivity, which dragged on until 1377, pre-cipitated an even stranger episode for the papacy: the aptly named Great (Western) Schism. At the death of Pope Urban V in 1370, a group of cardinals in Avignon and a separate group of cardinals in Rome each elected popes. Therefore, from 1370 to 1417, there were at least two—and sometimes three—different men staking a claim to the title. The situation was highly embarrassing, to say the least.

This was the church Catherine would be called to save.

After the plague, while those around them were stumbling along in a sort of spiritual abyss, the faith of the very devout Benincasa family remained rock-solid—despite the fact that the family fell on hard times after the oldest son's two business partners died, presumably of the plague. The deaths left Giacomo and his son unexpectedly responsible for a mountain of debt. But at least no one in the household had been infected, and, aside from some money trouble, daily life hummed along pretty much the way it always had. The home's atmosphere remained cheerful. While not oblivious to the somber state of affairs around them, no one doubted God's glory for a second.

The family was so faithful that, as long as Giacomo was alive, curse words were strictly forbidden under his roof. When Giacomo's daughter and Catherine's favorite sibling Bonaventura married a young Sienese man named Niccolo, she was stunned to hear her husband and his derelict friends engage in what biographers referred to as "foulmouthed" talk. In protest, she stopped eating, becoming dangerously ill after dropping too much weight. Her worried husband asked why she was refusing to eat. Her response: "In my father's house I was not used to listening to such words as I must hear here every day. You can be sure that if such indecent talk continues in our house you will live to see me waste to death." Apparently the well-meaning Niccolo immediately reformed—and the frail Bonaventura ate her way back to good health.

As a child, Catherine was rarely silent, her bubbly charm an almost irrepressible impulse. Indeed, Catherine was so merry that the family gave her the pet name of Euphrosyne, which is Greek for "joy" and is also the name of an early Christian saint. Early on, she was a natural leader who had no trouble drawing an audience. As a result, even as a very young child she was well known in her neighborhood, where daily life played out on the streets. Raymond of Capua, Catherine's close friend and first biographer, wrote that as a little girl her company was so sweet that it was indescribable: "only those who were ever with her can have any idea of it."

She and all her siblings would have been expected to help with chores such as fetching water at the nearby fountain. But children under eight also would have played with toys: balls, dolls, animals made from baked clay, spears made from sticks, wooden knights. Their main activities might have included running, skipping, chasing birds, climbing trees and wall-walking or some other balancing game.

Like the rest of her family, Catherine accepted prayer as a regular part of the daily routine, no different from fetching pails of clean water. She was meticulously devotional in everything she did, never failing to pause on each step as she climbed the stairs of her house to kneel and say an "Ave Maria." When friars passed the residence, she would drop what she was doing, race outside, lean down and kiss the traces of their footsteps. Instead of playing "house," she gathered friends together to play "convent," leading everyone in prayer as they all pretended to be nuns. Since Catherine couldn't read, much of her early religious education was derived from listening to Bible readings, as well as from staring at the dramatic and descriptive paintings in church and hearing the heroic tales of the early church martyrs. Like most girls of the medieval era, Catherine never enjoyed a formal education. For centuries, education was under the purview of the church, meaning almost no one outside of it learned to read and write. Even those of noble lineage in the early medieval era were illiterate. After Dante's *Divine Comedy* was printed in 1321, barely 10 percent of the Italian population could read it. By the late fourteenth century, some schools had been set up in important churches, in addition to some private lay schools, but they were generally for boys, though a few girls preparing to be nuns attended as well. Information about education during this period is sketchy, but Giovanni Villani, the Florentine chronicler, states that 8,000 to 10,000 boys in Florence had access to elementary education in 1339. Considering that there were about 90,000 people in Florence at the time, this would mean that 10 percent of the population was receiving some education at any given time. Villani also states that one-fourth of the boys would go on to one of six so-called *abacco* schools—or schools that focused on math and managing a business—in the city to learn practical skills.

Since Catherine was so amicable, neighbors always invited her to come over, making it extremely difficult for Lapa to keep tabs on her. Not only was Catherine exceptionally close to her pious sister, Bonaventura, she also developed a deep bond with an adored cousin, the ten-years-older Tommaso della Fonte, who was brought up in the Benincasa house. An earnest young man, Tommaso had his heart set on a religious vocation and would later become a Dominican friar and Catherine's first confessor. But aside from an almost defiant holiness, Catherine was in many ways just another normal little girl, playing childish games while being fawned over by her parents, siblings and neighbors.

And then a brief but otherworldly encounter during a walk with her brother Stefano changed Catherine's life—and the life of the Catholic Church—forever.

TWO

A First Glimpse of Christ

While one of the most transformative eras in history, the Middle Ages were also fraught with danger, especially for children. Historians estimate that 20 to 30 percent of children under seven died, although the actual figure is probably much higher. Children were particularly susceptible to smallpox, influenza, tuberculosis, whooping cough and other diseases. They also had to contend with a daily obstacle course of potential pitfalls. If having to dodge four-wheeled horse-drawn carts with no steering wasn't enough, children were also faced with open fires, uncovered wells and ditches and roaming farm animals. Life was challenging, and there was always something that needed doing. Children went to bed early, usually before sunset, and rose with the first light of day. Medieval parents were big believers in the biblical admonishment "Spare the rod and spoil the child." With so many dangers lurking about, a smack on the bottom or on the hands was seen as the most prudent form of childrearing. As soon as they could walk, children were expected to help their parents by doing simple chores such as fetching water from communal wells and chasing away birds from crop fields. Every child was assigned at least a few tasks in accordance with their ages. But, as noted, children also had time for play.

Little Catherine Benincasa was no different. She enjoyed a large circle of friends, both boys and girls, with whom she played games, but that never stopped her from lending a hand around the house. Her harmonious relationship with family and friends bore the imprint of her cheerful personality. She was kind, gentle and happy-go-lucky. While her father and brothers made and mixed dyes for coloring linen or woolen cloth in the cellar, she and her mother and sisters busied themselves in the big kitchen, no doubt surrounded by fumes arising from the dye vats. But then, in an instant, an extraordinary encounter punched a hole in the household's normality, and nothing would ever feel quite the same again.

This encounter was a mystical awakening that took place when Catherine was only six years old. The day had started out quite ordinary, with her mother asking Catherine and her brother Stefano to take something to Bonaventura, the sister who lived with her husband near the Porta di San Ansano, a fair distance away. Catherine adored Bonaventura and would have been elated by any excuse for a visit. No doubt Catherine and Stefano spent hours at their sister's house before heading back home again before nightfall. They walked as loose-limbed and carefree as ever, through the narrow streets and steep alleyways. They followed the same route, passing by the duomo and the hospital of Santa Maria della Scala before nearing the stairway that led down to their own Fontebranda neighborhood on the west side of the city. For some reason, though, Catherine fell behind. And then, without warning, something or someone stopped the little girl dead in her tracks. Suddenly, she looked up toward the sky, for no apparent reason.

Suspending all rational thought, she fixed her gaze on something no one else could see. She couldn't quite believe what was there: a vision of Christ on a throne, wearing a tiara and white papal robes and carrying a pastoral staff. It was the most beautiful sight. Jesus seemed to be staring straight at her. And he was smiling. Standing to his side were the Apostles Peter and Paul as well as John the Evangelist. Raymond of Capua wrote: "At the sight of all this the little girl remained rooted to the ground, gazing lovingly with unblinking eyes upon her Lord and Savior, who was revealing Himself to her in this way in order to captivate her love. Then, gazing straight at her with eyes full of majesty, and smiling most lovingly, He raised His right hand over her, made the sign of the cross of salvation like a priest, and graciously gave her His eternal benediction."

Surrounded in the street by animals and passersby, Catherine froze like a statue as if her feet had taken root, with her head tilted upward. Stunned but ecstatic, she forgot everything else, basking in the love of God as it rained down upon her, seeping into her very soul. And she would have stayed that way all night if her impatient brother hadn't come running over to grab her hand, which shook her out of her trance. He cried out, "What are you doing? We have to go." She replied, "If you could see what I can you would not be so cruel and disturb me out of this lovely vision." She looked toward the sky again and then burst into tears when she realized there was no longer anything to see. The apparition had disappeared. She begged her brother not to tell their parents or anyone else what had happened. Even then, she seemed to realize that the celestial scene was a gift for her and her alone, and she wanted to keep it her own very big secret, at least for the time being. Christ had chosen only her. He seemed pleased with her. He had initiated only her.

An interesting aside is that, according to Raymond, Catherine apparently saw Christ wearing papal vestments. It's unusual in religious imagery to depict Christ wearing papal robes while sitting on a throne. No one has determined why Catherine, as such a young child, would envision such a scene. But for the rest of her life, loyalty to the pope would be on a par with loyalty to Christ.

After the vision, Catherine returned home, engulfed in sadness and berating herself for her inattentiveness, believing it was her neglect that had made Jesus disappear. One early account said this: "From this moment, she was always tormented from inside, fearful, conscientious, and afraid of falling into sin, as much as was possible for a girl of her age." She vowed to beat her body and mind into submission, the beginning of a lifelong regimen of strict self-discipline. Indeed, that flash of insight on that otherwise ordinary afternoon along the road had turned her world on its head. Catherine no longer felt like a little girl of six, but more like a woman with profound maturity. From that day forward, she concerned herself only with those things that pertained to God. Everything else was cast aside. Instead of playing childish games, she filled her free time with additional prayer and meditation. The chatty little girl who once talked her neighbors' ears off grew increasingly quiet and introspective. She also ate less, suddenly finding that she needed barely any food to sustain her— a bizarre about-face for a young girl who had spent most days working companionably alongside her mother, cooking and eating large meals in the kitchen. Despite the sudden changes in her behavior, her new persona would prove to be just as alluring as her old one as she again attracted a band of pint-sized disciples. They followed her around, hard on her heels, never tiring of repeating the Our Father and Hail Mary on her orders. "Inspired by her example, a number of other little girls of her own age gathered round her, eager to hear her talk about salvation and to imitate her as best they could," Raymond wrote. Her mystical life had begun.

Historically, the range of people reporting mystical episodes has been vast—including popes, actors, saints, shamans and Old Testament prophets. Some have been religious—some not. Almost all, though, have reported the same intense experience as Catherine of being lifted out of themselves by some kind of powerful spiritual vision or force.

Far from being a new phenomenon, mysticism is a current that has run through the Catholic Church since the third century and continues to this day. Like other mystics, Catherine willfully sought a direct relationship to God through prayer and devotion. Always, her overwhelming desire was to remain united with him. Theologian Hilda C. Graef wrote in her 1948 book, *The Way of the Mystics:* "It is one of the most consoling facts that mystics seem to flourish especially in turbulent times. There is no more striking an example of the mystic life lived in the turmoil of the world than that of St. Catherine of Siena. For it is her mystic life that gives us the explanation of her extraordinary power over men and women."

Later, in her book *The Dialogue,* Catherine claimed that the ability to communicate with God and create Christian doctrine would not be possible without her mystical experiences. "The tongue cannot describe it, but the holy doctors have shown it well when, enlightened by this glorious light [grace], they explained Holy Scripture . . . the glorious Thomas Aquinas . . . gained his knowledge more from the study of prayer and the lifting up of his mind and the light of understanding than from human study," she wrote.

These days, the Catholic Church reacts to reports of supernatural visions with a mixture of enthusiasm and skepticism. Mystics can inspire believers, but Catholic leaders are also wary of hoaxes. Many hundreds of visions have been reported in recent centuries. Some have been disregarded. But some have precipitated vast spiritual movements.

In the Middle Ages, there were literally dozens of female visionaries in Italy. Agnes of Montepulciano, who lived from 1268 to 1317, saw the Virgin Mary, who allowed her to hold the baby Jesus. Margaret of Cortona, who lived from 1247 to 1297, was visited by Jesus after she converted and became a Third Order Franciscan, or one of those following St. Francis of Assisi in prayer and action. And Christianity is not alone in citing mystical experiences as the genesis of spiritual practices. Islam, Judaism, Buddhism, Hinduism and Shamanism all can be seen as evolving from an original "epiphany"—or primary mystical experience. Moses personally experienced the Divine in a burning bush, Jesus in the desert, Muhammad in a cave and the Buddha under a Bodhi tree. The prophet Ezekiel had a vision of God's chariot and then rode into heaven on it. As Søren Kierkegaard put it, "Just as in earthly life, lovers long for the moment when they are able to breathe forth their love for each other, to let their souls bend in a soft whisper, so the mystic longs for the moment when in prayer, he can, as it were, creep into God."

In the history of the Catholic Church, no era has been lacking in mystics. From the age of seven St. Faustina Kowalska, a Polish nun born in 1905, recounted seeing Christ dozens of times. In one of her most interesting recollections, she described dancing at a party as a 20-year-old when Jesus appeared to her, covered with wounds. Everything surrounding her faded away, and she saw only him. He asked her, "How long shall I put up with you and how long will you keep putting me off?" Exuberant, she impulsively ran off to pray after the incident and joined a convent shortly afterward. More recently, the Venezuelan mystic Maria Esperanza, who predicted many major twentieth-century events in advance, described seeing dozens of apparitions of Mary before her death in 2004. Born in 1928, she reportedly had the ability to heal and levitate. So revered is Esperanza that, in 2010, the case for her beatification and canonization was opened, the first step in a lengthy process to make her a saint.

When interviewed in 2014 about whether he'd ever had a mystical experience, Father Alfredo White, an expert on St. Catherine who lives in Siena, confessed, "No, I have not had a mystical experience. I'm still too much of a sinner."

Few people are as renowned for their work on the subject of mysticism as the English writer Evelyn Underhill. Published in 1911, her book *Mysticism* remains the classic in its field. For Underhill, mysticism is the process by which one's individual soul moves toward complete union with the "absolute." Underhill said that there are key stages that mark the progress of any mystic: awakening, purification, illumination, voices and visions, contemplation and introversion, ecstasy and rapture, the dark night of the soul and union with the divine. In the first stage—awakening—one suddenly wakes up to a world filled with splendor in which everything is in perfect harmony with everything else.

Catherine's awakening was that first vision, after which she exhibited a spiritual energy that made others surrender to her influence so that she was rarely without companions. And yet—like most young mystics—what the popular young girl really pined for was solitude. Again and again, she tried to slip away from her little flock and become like the desert hermits she'd heard so much about who lived alone in caves, with little food and almost no material goods, just outside Siena's walls. One day she went so far as to pack a loaf of bread and hike toward her sister Bonaventura's house. Rather than stop in, though, she kept going, making her way beyond the city walls and deep into the countryside, past olive groves and verdant hills. Eventually she found a cave to her liking and settled in under a rock overhang to pray—just as if she were a hermit. At that moment, Catherine was lifted into the air, all the while fervently expressing her love of God, according to Raymond's account. Initially believing this to be the work of the devil, she prayed even more earnestly. But again, she felt as though she were floating close to the roof. She ultimately decided that the episode actually had nothing whatsoever to do with the devil, but rather was a sign that her prayers were getting through to God, and that she was truly bonding with the Deity. When she woke from her trance, she found herself on her knees on the ground. The hour was precisely 3:00 p.m., the same time Jesus died on the cross. Euphoric, she could have gone on praying the entire night. But she knew her parents would worry and so—still the dutiful daughter—she returned home that evening. The incident was just further confirmation to her that she was different from everyone else in her family. And she was coming to realize that she would probably have to fight to preserve this newfound individuality.

For Giacomo and Lapa, so used to their children's obedience, Catherine was becoming a difficult child to bring up. Once, when she was around ten, Lapa told her to go to church and ask the priest to say a Mass in honor of St. Anthony, the patron saint of finding lost things or people. Delighted at any opportunity to serve God, Catherine went scampering off. She found the priest and did as she was told but then stayed on for the celebration of Mass. Lapa, who had wanted her to return home as soon as she had finished talking to the priest, scolded Catherine, saying, "Cursed be the chatterers who said you would never come back." Catherine replied, "Lady, mother, when I don't do what you tell me to do, or go too far, beat me as much as you like . . . but I beg you not to let my failings make your tongue run away with you and make you start cursing the neighbors, whoever they may be, because this doesn't suit anyone of your age and it causes me very great pain." Needless to say, Lapa stared at her daughter and said nothing.

Girls during this era were typically married off as soon as they were physically able to consummate a sexual relationship, usually around the age of 12 or 13. For a medieval Sienese family like Catherine's, the marriage of a daughter was more than just a matter of finding a suitable mate. It was a way to solidify and lift up the fortunes and futures of every member of the household. Biographer Sigrid Undset noted that Catherine's obstinacy would have been incredibly problematic for her parents. "For the people of the Middle Ages, the family was still the most powerful protector of the rights and welfare of the individual. In a time so full of unrest and disturbance, the protection a man could expect from the community—whether state or town—was at the best uncertain," she writes. "But a group consisting of fathers, sons, and sons-in-law who held fast together and faithfully defended their common interests at least promised a certain amount of security." Women who did not marry were not permitted to live independently. They weren't even allowed to go out on their own. Usually, they lived in the homes of male relatives—or joined a convent.

But unbeknownst to her family, Catherine had called on the Virgin Mary at the age of seven to help her commit herself completely to Jesus. Raymond described this as a "vow of virginity." According to him, Catherine had said: "Give me as my Spouse the One I long for from my inmost heart, your own all-holy and only Son, our Lord Jesus Christ; and I promise him and promise you that to no other spouse will I ever give myself, but in my own humble measure I too will keep my virginity forever spotless for him."

No doubt Catherine's pledge had more to do with her whole-hearted commitment to Christ and less to do with sex. As she entered her teen years, Catherine's family begged her to dress more like a young woman looking to lure a husband. Lapa enlisted the help of her married daughter Bonaventura to persuade Catherine to make herself more desirable. As a pious woman, and Catherine's favorite sister, Bonaventura was a formidable ally. If Catherine was going to listen to anyone, it would be she. And she did—at least at first. Because she truly loved her mother and her sister, her desire to appease them initially eclipsed her religious fervor, and, for a time, Catherine tried to make herself more presentable. She even agreed to lighten her hair—most likely a light brown—to a yellowish color that was so prized during this time period. For a few weeks, Catherine was content with all this, pleased to be spending so much time with her sister. But eventually all the fuss only made Catherine uncomfortable and it wasn't long before she bristled any time the notion of marriage was brought up. When her mother tried to dress her up in new clothing, she refused. It got so bad that any time a male caller came around, she was nowhere to be found. According to Raymond, when she really wanted to avoid people, especially men, she ascended the stairs with a miraculous quickness, thanks to help from the Lord, who lifted her up in the air so that her feet no longer touched the stairs. Catherine was forever mindful of the private vow of virginity she had made to Mary at the age of seven.

Although her family knew nothing of her vow of virginity, Catherine's much-loved older cousin, Tommaso, did. His advice was to meet her parents' resoluteness with such obstinacy that they'd have no choice but to finally give up. He suggested a dramatic manifestation of defiance: cutting off her long hair, which was perhaps her greatest physical asset. And so she did just that.

She cropped off her lovely locks close to her scalp and then tied a little veil over her head. As it was not customary for an unmarried woman to cover her hair, Lapa demanded to know what was going on as soon as she saw her. Ripping off the veil, Lapa sobbed at the sight of her nearly bald head. Her wails grew so loud that Catherine's father and brothers dropped everything and came rushing in. They, too, were startled by what they saw. After all, the future of the family and its business rested on the making of advantageous marriages. From all accounts, Catherine was not unattractive, but she also was not wildly pretty. Her long hair may have been the only physical attribute working in her favor.

So angry was Lapa that she swiftly got rid of her housemaid and ordered Catherine to be the new family servant. The aim was to so overwhelm her with chores that she wouldn't have time for praying or anything else. Lapa also took away her little bedroom and made her sleep in a corner of the kitchen, leaving Catherine with almost no privacy. Although the issue drove a wedge between her and her mother, Catherine managed to take the punishment in stride and found joy in serving others. Raymond wrote that she made a kind of game out of it, imagining that her father was Jesus, her mother the Virgin Mary, her brothers apostles and the kitchen a sanctuary. As such, she performed her daily duties contentedly by seeing her punishment as a catalyst for new spiritual growth. She later told Raymond how she had finally figured out the way to achieve solace and solitude even in the midst of chaos. "Build an inner cell in your soul and never leave it," she said. Writing to a young widow years later, Catherine explained that people must make two homes for themselves: one is their actual home and the other is "a spiritual home which you carry with you always, the cell of true self-knowledge where you find within yourself knowledge of God's goodness."

We're not sure how long the debate about Catherine's future dragged on. But according to early biographers, Mary Magdalene, once a woman of great wealth who turned into a repentant sinner, was a role model for Catherine starting around this time. Paintings of this exceptional woman, so prominent in all of the Gospels, would have been on display in Siena's churches. Lapa warned Catherine that her lack of hair changed nothing in the long run and that—as soon as it grew back—the search for a suitable spouse would resume. Despite this, and despite the ongoing harassment by her brothers, Catherine gleefully performed her chores day and night without a single complaint. Frustrated, Lapa made a last-ditch effort to force her daughter to act like other girls her age by taking her to the fashionable natural hot springs in Vignoni about 30 miles south of Siena. The baths were considered a real treat that any young woman would have relished. But once there, Catherine asked to bathe alone. Her mother agreed, thinking her daughter just wanted some privacy. Catherine had other ideas, however. Instead of going to the pools with the pleasantly warm water, she went to the precise spot where the water entered the pool, scalding hot. She inflicted massive pain on herself by exposing her skin to the water while imagining she was enduring the torments of hell. When Lapa found her and discovered that her skin was red and wrinkled from the blistering water, she was beside herself. Later, when Raymond heard about the incident, he asked Catherine how she withstood such hot water. She replied that the Lord had filled her soul with such heavenly consolation that she was happy even in the midst of her pain.

Lapa was dismayed by her daughter's behavior, but she soon had an even greater crisis to deal with. In August 1362, when Catherine was 15, Bonaventura and her baby died in childbirth.

The entire family was devastated. Catherine, too, was consumed by grief. History doesn't reveal exactly what went wrong, only that God sent word to Catherine years later that her sister—unknowingly an obstacle to Catherine's complete commitment to her bridegroom Christ—had gone to heaven after serving a very short stint in purgatory. Giacomo and Lapa had lost a daughter, but there were still three other unmarried girls in the family—Lisa, Catherine and Giovanna. It would have been customary for their attention to naturally shift next to Lisa, the oldest daughter after Bonaventura's death. But for whatever reason, that wasn't the case. Details surrounding the sisters are murky. Some accounts have suggested that Giacomo and Lapa tried to match Catherine with Bonaventura's widowed husband, Niccolo de Giovanni Tegliacci. For Catherine, Niccolo was an especially upsetting prospect due to his previous penchant for indecent language.

With the support of Tommaso, who by now was a Dominican priest, Catherine finally found the courage to take a real stand against her family. "It is not a long time since you first took counsel, and began negotiations, as you said, to have me married off as the bride of some mere mortal man," Raymond recorded Catherine telling her parents.

> The very thought of this filled me with loathing, as I made plain to you in many silent ways, whose meaning, however, was unmistakable. But God has commanded us to honor our father and mother, and for the reverence due to them I have never bluntly spoken out my mind until now. But the time has come when I can be silent no longer. I will lay bare my heart to you and say out plain and straight what I am resolved to do. It is no newfound purpose that I speak of, but one that has been early known to me, and firmly willed, from childhood.

Already when I was a child, I made a vow of virginity, not, however, in the way a child would do, but after long consideration and acting on solid grounds. I made this vow to my Lord and Savior Jesus Christ, and to his glorious mother. I promised them that never would I take another spouse but him alone. And now in the course of time, as the Lord himself had willed it, I have arrived at a mature age and mature knowledge. Take notice, then, that my resolution is so firm in this regard that it would be easier to soften the very rock than to move my heart a hairsbreadth from its holy purpose. The more you try to do so, the more you will discover that you are only wasting your time. I must obey God rather than man.

At the end of Catherine's speech, some family members wept. Others, no doubt, simply sat with their mouths open. Yes, they were disappointed. But they also were taken aback. Here was their sweet sister—their sweet daughter—making a bullheaded statement of independence. Even Lapa, with whom Catherine had so often clashed, had to respect her spunk. In the Middle Ages, a young boy making such a bold declaration to his parents would have raised eyebrows. For a young girl to do it was absolutely unimaginable. Catherine, though, stood her ground and held her own.

Giacomo steadied himself and found his voice. As the head of the family, it was his authority that Catherine was chiefly defying. Giacomo was a reasonable man who loved his family deeply, and he announced that he would accept Catherine's vow, even urging her to be faithful to it. He promised that the family would back off any attempts to marry her off and then instructed Lapa and the others to leave her in peace so that she could pray whenever and wherever she wanted. And so, with that, Catherine was back in her family's good graces.

Until the day she died, Catherine would berate herself for her brief flirtation with arrogance. Somewhat bizarrely, she confessed to Raymond years later the massive "sin" she had committed by allowing herself to be dolled up and paraded around by her mother and sister, albeit briefly. What disturbed Catherine even more was that she had allowed herself to love her sister more than God. For the rest of her life, she would try to exorcise this momentary lapse in judgment—this demon—through severe acts of penance. Raymond conceded that there might have been a bit of excess but that, in his view, it had been so inconsequential that it surely wasn't important enough to displease God. At that, an exasperated Catherine raised her head upward and exclaimed, "Oh, Lord God, what kind of a spiritual father is this you have given me, who finds excuses for my sins!" She told Raymond: "Father, is this vile miserable creature who has received so many graces from her Creator without any labor or merit on her own part supposed to spend her time beautifying her putrid flesh to deceive some poor mortal? I don't believe so . . . that hell itself would have been a sufficient punishment for me if the divine pity had not had mercy on me." Raymond had no idea how to react. Only then did he realize how high Catherine set the bar for herself. In *The Dialogue* Catherine wrote often of the evilness of pride. "And who is hurt by the offspring of pride? Only your neighbors. For you harm them when your exalted opinion of yourself leads you to consider yourself superior and therefore to despise them," she said. "And if pride is in a position of authority, it gives birth to injustice and cruelty, and becomes a dealer in human flesh."

Within her own family, Giacomo seems to have understood Catherine and the reasons for her resoluteness best. As the days wore on, he grew more and more convinced that his daughter was guided not by some kind of youthful capriciousness, but by a special and genuine spirituality. And if any doubts remained, they were shattered when, one day, Giacomo accidentally stumbled upon a kneeling Catherine deep in prayer in her brother Stefano's room. As he watched from outside the door, he saw a lovely white dove poised above her head. When he approached, it flew out the window. He asked Catherine about it, but she had seen nothing. He knew right then and there that she was destined for great things.

Only now was Catherine finally ready and able to take her next radical step in her response to God's calling.

THREE

Kiss Me with a Kiss of Your Mouth

An extraordinary episode was soon to occur in the young Catherine's life, a mystical experience known as the "spiritual espousal." Of course, many early Christian women were wed to Christ through a mystical marriage. The list begins with another Catherine—this one a revered martyr of the fourth century born into a noble family from Alexandria, Egypt. A young lady of striking beauty, St. Catherine of Alexandria was said to prefer studying—especially the philosophy of Plato—to marriage. Though she was sought by many suitors, she vowed to her parents to marry only if she could find a man who "surpassed her in wisdom, wealth, illustriousness and beauty." That led, as tradition tells it, to her discovery of Christ. Although raised a pagan, she turned to Christianity during her teenage years after receiving a vision of the Virgin Mary and Christ in which Mary placed a ring on her finger, signaling Catherine's mystical marriage to Jesus. Catherine reportedly exclaimed: "His beauty was more radiant than the shining of the sun, His wisdom governed all creation, and His riches were spread throughout all the world." Finally, she had met her match.

Another remarkable self-proclaimed spiritual bride of Christ was Margery Kempe, who lived around the same time as Catherine of Siena. But Margery's story has a twist. Born in England in 1373, Margery married John Kempe when she was about 20. Over the next two decades, she gave birth to 14 children, living an ordinary middle-class life and even overseeing her own brewing business. But she began to receive visions of Jesus after the birth of her first child and, around age 40, vowed to live a celibate life alongside her husband while devoting her heart and soul completely to Christ. She too enjoyed a mystical marriage when, again in a vision, Jesus commanded her to commission a ring, and to have it engraved with "Jesus is my love." Margery took this to be a wedding ring and apparently, from that moment on, she was so enamored of Christ's masculinity that she cried any time she saw a boy baby. In *The Book of Margery Kempe* she wrote about her call to be God's wife and the impact it had on her earthly marriage. Any pleasure she derived from her carnal relationship with John, she said, ran a distant second to the joy and closeness she luxuriated in in her relationship with God. "Forsooth, I would rather see you being slain, than that we should turn again to our uncleanness," she told her husband. In addition to Margery, many other mystical brides burst onto the scene during the Middle Ages, composing spiritual writings that guided both male and female readers across Europe. The increasing number of prophetesses included St. Teresa of Ávila, who remains one of the most influential saints of our century as well as of her own sixteenth century. Teresa and the others made their voices known, held sway over countless followers—men included—and rejoiced in their own mystical marriages. These women often spoke of being "led" by Christ, not as impotent or inferior creatures, but rather as self-assured devotees who had no doubts about their abilities or the path they were on. Although their hearts belonged to God, these women were fiercely independent, and their actions and writings have inspired many generations of believers.

In one of the most haunting texts in the tradition of female mysticism, Teresa spoke of her own union with Christ: "It pleased the Lord that I should sometimes see the following vision. I would see beside me, on my left hand, an angel in bodily form . . . In his hands I saw a great golden spear, and at the iron tip there appeared to be a point of fire. This he plunged into my heart several times so that it penetrated my entrails. When he drew it out I felt that he took them with it, and left me utterly consumed with a great love for God . . . The sweetness caused by this intense pain is so extreme that one cannot possibly wish it to cease, nor will one's soul be content with anything less than God."

Teresa was a spiritual late bloomer, only becoming serious about her faith around age 40. As one author of several books on Teresa said, her years of deep prayer continue to enrich Christians everywhere: "Teresa describes coherently a God who desires intimate companionship and collaboration from us and with us." And she was notorious for her sense of humor. Once a stunned friend stumbled upon Teresa gorging herself on a partridge, considered a particular delicacy at the time, and asked, "What would people think?" Teresa famously replied, "Let them think whatever they want. There's a time for penance, and there's a time for partridge."

Simone de Beauvoir placed St. Catherine of Siena and St. Teresa of Ávila on the same pedestal. In her book *The Second Sex*, she called them both "saintly souls, beyond any physiological condition; their lay life and their mystical life, their actions and their writings, rise to heights that few men ever attain."

The concept of being married to Christ gave Catherine, Teresa and other medieval women a distinct advantage over men at a time when women were supposed to stay subservient and keep quiet. While males were higher up on the societal ladder of command, there was one rung they'd never be able to reach: marriage with Jesus. As a result, the spiritual lives of men were much less intimate, much less profound. As a group, women visionaries in the Middle Ages found meaning in a unique spirituality and therefore shared a heightened sense of well-being that was all their own. Recognized as being guardians of the transcendent, many more women than men experienced ecstatic rapture and the exclusive preview of heaven that came along with it. As Caroline Walker Bynum wrote in her 1987 *Holy Feast and Holy Fast,* "Men were authoritative by office or ordination; women's religious power derived from inspiration, from ecstatic visitation . . . there is much evidence that religious men in the thirteenth, fourteenth, and fifteenth centuries were fascinated by women—both by the female visionaries who became, through their very lowliness, the mouthpieces of God on high and by the ordinary mothers, housewives, laundresses, and maidservants who were signs of the depths to which Jesus stooped in redeeming humankind."

Throughout the Bible, various passages refer to mystical marriage, equating the believer's relationship with the Lord to that of a bride with her betrothed. One of Catherine of Siena's favorite New Testament authors, Paul, wrote to the Corinthians, "For I am jealous over you with a godly jealousy: for I have espoused you to one husband that I may present [you as] a chaste virgin to Christ." And: "But he who is joined to the Lord is one spirit with him." Sprinkled throughout the Bible, these references characterize marriage between husband and wife as the creation of one flesh and marriage between Christ and a believer as the creation of one spirit.

Catherine of Siena had already become so smitten with Christ by the age of seven that she had consecrated her virginity to him. "Give me as husband Him whom I desire with all the power of my soul . . . and I promise Him and you that I will never choose myself another husband," she said. Although historians never wrote about this, while growing up she most likely at least toyed with the idea of becoming a nun, someone married to Christ, anchored by near-constant prayer. But the prospect of being sheltered from the outside world—as all nuns of that era were—may not have piqued the interest of the extroverted Catherine, who eventually wanted to take her bold prophetic voice on the road. Fortunately for her, there was another avenue she could take that would be more to her liking. She could become a tertiary, or lay member, of a spiritual community that was committed to a more religious schedule of life but not bound by formal vows. Members did not live in convents, but in their home, buoyed by the charism and example of a supportive group of compatible Christians. Both the Franciscans and the Dominicans had male and female tertiaries. In Siena, the Dominican women who abided by certain rules but remained living in their own homes were called the Mantellate because of their distinctive religious habit—a black mantle worn over a white tunic.

As Catherine matured into a more thoughtful young woman, she would have sought out some way to ratify her inner commitment to Christ through an alliance with like-minded people. Since she was a little girl, she'd been in love with the idea of becoming a Dominican like her beloved cousin Tommaso. Her aunt Agnes, too, was a member. And still there was another draw: the Mantellate offered a way to skirt her family's expectations that she marry and have children. Raymond wrote about how Catherine was also inspired by a dream in which St. Dominic appeared to her, holding in his hands the habit worn by the tertiaries in addition to a white lily. Dominic told her, "Dearest daughter, be of good courage; do not lose heart, no matter what the odds against you. Be assured that you will one day wear this habit which you long for." In her *Dialogue*, Catherine described Dominic as "an apostle of the world" who spread God's word wherever he went, "dispelling darkness and giving light." Catherine often expressed a desire to imitate Dominic, and, ten years after her death, she was depicted holding a lily in Andrea Vanni's fresco, a painting that still hangs in the west chapel of Siena's Basilica of San Domenico.

But one thing stood in the way of Catherine's joining the Mantellate: almost all the members were older widows.

Catherine conferred with Tommaso, who by now had become a highly valued first confessor. In the Middle Ages, a particularly religious woman such as Catherine would have had a man—a confessor—supervising her devotions and thereby becoming an eyewitness to her life. Tommaso was certain the challenge wasn't insurmountable and that the Mantellate would have to accept Catherine as her noble and pious character was beyond reproach. But when she mentioned the idea to Lapa, her mother vehemently opposed it, arguing that she was far too young. Members of the Mantellate were mature women, she contended, not fresh-faced adolescents. And because members were allowed to live at home—where they might be subject to earthly temptations—they had to have the maturity to resist all impure enticements. There was no way they'd welcome a teenager into the insularity of such a picky family. At first, Lapa was right. The Mantellate refused to receive her. But nearly overnight Catherine became alarmingly ill, possibly with smallpox. Lapa sat by Catherine's bed and nursed her around the clock, employing every conventional tactic she could think of to make her well again. Nothing worked. And nothing ever would work, Catherine told her mother, except for one thing—acceptance into the Mantellate. Desperate, Lapa would have done anything to help her sick child. And so she went to the Mantellate, imploring its members to allow Catherine to join. Lapa was nothing if not a good talker, and eventually she wore them down. They agreed to at least mull the matter over, as much to appease Lapa as Catherine. There was only one minor impediment to overcome. If Catherine were unusually beautiful, they wouldn't want to accept her. Lapa was cunning enough to invite the women to come and find out for themselves. Lapa knew that her poor Catherine, at home with her face swollen underneath hideous red splotches, wasn't even remotely attractive.

The Mantellate singled out a few of its more experienced and trustworthy women to call upon her. They showed up, and, within minutes, the women were in complete agreement: Catherine was anything but pretty. But after they had spoken with her for a while, it was the beauty and purity of her spirit that shone through. After a brief consultation, the Mantellate unanimously agreed that Catherine would be welcomed into the Third Order of St. Dominic as one of the Sisters of Penitence. When Lapa broke the news to her daughter, Catherine wept with relief. She asked God to be well again, and, within days, she had fully recovered. She received the habit, possibly in 1363, when she was 17. Oddly enough, though, she never fully abided by the same rules adhered to by all the other Mantellate members, despite how much she had wanted to be one of them. Perhaps because of her stellar reputation both inside and outside the Mantellate, no one seemed to mind. As the years went on, she often went about town unchaperoned—which no other self-respecting member of the Mantellate would have done at the time—circulating freely with men in direct violation of the group's edicts. She also strayed far from home whereas others did not. Members of the Mantellate also were required to adhere to ecclesiastically regulated prayer several times a day. Since few could read, this meant the memorization and recitation of a certain number of Paternosters and Ave Marias in place of the Latin psalms. Catherine very quickly grew tired of the repetitiveness as she preferred creative prayer that was more than just rote learning.

Historical scholars still have mixed views when it comes to the chronology of her Mantellate membership and other major life events. But there is one occurrence for which they are sure of the date. On April 18, 1363, Catherine's younger sister, Giovanna, died at the age of 14. The cause of death is not recorded. Catherine and Lapa were both profoundly sad, a grief that inevitably bound the two of them together.

After joining the Dominicans, Catherine continued to live in the family home on Via dei Tintori, spending most of her time praying alone in a nine-by-three-foot room with one small window—what Catherine's followers later referred to as her "cell"—set aside for her under a flight of stairs. It contained nothing but a bed made from planks of wood, some sort of tallow or wax candle, and a crucifix on the wall. But for her it was perfect, and at last she had what she so desired: a place to retreat and enjoy the blissful oblivion of solitude—with her parents' blessing. For a large middle-class family in the fourteenth century, a room of one's own was quite the extravagance. Space was at a particular premium inside the Benincasa household at this time because Catherine's two oldest brothers were also living there, along with their wives and children.

For Catherine, her induction into the Mantellate marked the beginning of a period of almost unbelievable austerity and mystical communion with Christ. Divine visitations became increasingly common, giving Catherine less and less of a reason to leave her cell. She cut herself off from all worldly connections, vacating her small quarters only to attend early Mass at the nearby Dominican church. During the day, when the rest of her family was out and about, she hunkered down in her room. When she did go out, it was typically at night, and then only because she wanted to catch a glimpse of the stars in the sky, which she imagined to be a cloak worn by God. As she put it, "The garment of yours is covered with stars, all the different virtues, for we can have no patience without the stars of all the virtues along with the night of self-knowledge, which is a sort of moonlight." The words—written much later—sum up the objectives of her eremitic years. In her understanding, self-knowledge was something more than just psychological insight. It was a matter of knowing one's place in the eyes of God. Only when she allowed God's love to overwhelm her did she discover her unimportance. To Catherine, we are nothing in the face of God's perfection. Only our "true" actual self is a reflection of God's greatness.

In keeping with her ascetic lifestyle, Catherine relied for sustenance almost exclusively on herbs, water and bread—and Holy Communion. Indeed, the perfect meal for her was always the Eucharist. After receiving it, she often collapsed into a state of ecstasy, sometimes for hours at a time. Witnesses said her arms and legs became stiff, as if she were frozen in place. Her facial features, in repose, were transfixed on something not apparent to anyone else in the room, and she lost all sense of time and place. After Mass ended, the other worshipers would depart, invariably leaving Catherine behind. Inevitably, an irked lay brother waiting impatiently to lock up the church would come along, clanging his keys as a not-so-subtle sign that it was time for her to go. These men must have hated to see her coming. Once a lay brother shouted "Catherine" into her ears while also pinching her arms in an effort to snap her back to reality. When that didn't work, he picked her up and deposited her in a heap outside the churchyard's gate. After lying for a while on the ground in the heat of the noontime sun, she came to her senses and walked home.

Catherine never cared a whit about others' opinions of her. Her time of solitude fed her spiritually, and she was more engaged with Christ and less concerned with everyone else. Raymond said that, during the three years she spent in the cell, Christ became such a ubiquitous presence that "it would be hard to find two people who spent their time so constantly in each other's company as these two did." Tommaso di Antonio Nacci Caffarini, one of Catherine's earliest followers, said that the two would speak like "the father with the daughter or like the most diligent teacher with his best disciple." Raymond noted that it was during this period that God famously told her, "Do you know, O daughter, who you are and who I am? You are she who is not, and I am he who is." This fundamental theological insight—that self-love is the root from which every evil grows—would become the bedrock of her faith and teachings. Catherine's goal throughout her life would be to rid herself and others of self-centeredness.

Not only was Catherine visited by Christ in her cell, but she also was visited by unbidden demons. Images of attractive young men would suddenly appear out of nowhere, swirling in front of her face, trying to entice her, tempt her and beseech her to walk with them beyond the city's walls. Modern psychologists might argue that these demonic temptations were simply a vivid imagination at work inside a young woman harboring doubts about the lonesome path she was taking. But later Catherine was very specific when recalling the speech made by the devil to try to lure her over to his side.

What is the point of all this affliction? What will all these excruciating sufferings bring you in the long run? Do you imagine you can keep them up forever? Impossible! Unless you want to kill yourself and end up as a suicide. Be wise in time. Drop this nonsense before it leads to a complete breakdown. It is not yet too late to enjoy the delights which life can offer. The resilience of youth is on your side; your body can win back its freshness and vigor. Live the life that other women do. Take a husband. Be a mother of children. Bow to the law of human nature to increase and multiply. None of this can hinder the fulfillment of your desire of pleasing God. Have not saintly women been wives and mothers? Think of Sarah and Rebecca. Why should you make yourself an exception, taking on a kind of life in which you will never be able to persevere?

One day, after the devil had been particularly vehement in his assault on her senses, Catherine apparently declared, "I have made the choice of suffering as the well-spring of my strength. It is no hardship for me, but rather a delight, to endure for my Savior's name all you have been inflicting on me, and more besides, for as long as it shall please his Majesty." And with that, the demons finally fled her cell and the room was bathed in a dazzling, luminous light. Catherine was able to make out only one shape: an outline of Christ, nailed to the cross. He said to her, "My daughter Catherine, look at what I have suffered for your sake. Do not take it hard, then, when you too must suffer something for my sake." When she heard the word "daughter," Catherine was filled with joy, believing it proved Christ's amazing love for her. As time went on, Catherine would refer to someone as a son or daughter of God whenever she wanted to illustrate the ultimate ranking on the progression toward spiritual maturity.

In total, Catherine spent three years living in her cell, almost as a hermit, during which time her acts of penance only became more extreme. She exchanged words with almost no one but God and her confessor, Tommaso. She ate almost nothing and slept on wooden boards, with a stone as her pillow. She claimed that she survived on only a half hour of sleep every two days. She also flagellated herself three times a day until she drew blood and wore a hair shirt of coarse animal pelt next to her skin. When it became impossible to clean, she gave it up for an even more painful iron chain, which she wrapped around her waist. Raymond wrote that during one year, "From [Lent] until the feast of the Ascension of our Lord," a period of about 80 days, "she kept a complete fast, taking all that time no bodily food or drink whatsoever." On Ascension Day, she permitted herself just a few bites of vegetables. All this nearly drove Lapa mad with worry. Whenever she came upon Catherine sleeping on bare boards, she would carry her off and into her own room, where she forced her to lie down in bed beside her. But Catherine only went through the motions. After Lapa fell asleep, she would get up and tiptoe back to her own cell. Catherine was so determined to suffer that she took a few pieces of wood and surreptitiously placed them under the sheets in her mother's bed so that, even when she was next to Lapa, she might feel as tortured as possible. After a few days, though, her dismayed mother always discovered the ruse. She said, "As far as I can see, I am wasting my time. You are getting more and more obstinate about these principles of yours, so I might just as well close my eyes to them and let you sleep how and where you please." Other times, Lapa lashed out at her daughter for purposely scourging herself. She said, "I can see you dying before my very eyes! You'll kill yourself, of a truth you will. Oh, mercy me, who wants to take my daughter away? Who is bringing all these misfortunes upon me?" The woman would shriek so loud that even the neighbors would come running. Eventually, though, Lapa came to realize she'd never beat her daughter in a battle of wills. Catherine never faltered in her resolve, no matter how often others tried to trip her up. Raymond wrote about how, years later, he once sprinkled a bit of sugar into her water when she wasn't looking, in order to build up her strength. She tasted the sweetness immediately and angrily scolded him, "It seems to me you want to take away the little bit of life I still have left!" He asked what she meant and learned that she had grown so used to eating food without sugar that sweet things had become akin to poison to her. The same was true of meat.

In the medieval era, "the more you were like Jesus in his sufferings, the holier you were and the better," Suzanne Noffke, who translated and edited Catherine's letters, told the *New York Times* in 1999. "She very much wanted martyrdom." Catherine's desire for death and suffering most likely drew on the recirculated stories of those who endured regular persecution at the hands of the Roman authorities during the first three centuries of Christianity. Many of these devotional models who suffered and died for their faith during that time were women. It was veneration for this kind of persecution that spawned the cult of the saint so many years later. These courageous women, known for their purity of heart under great duress, acted as role models for those, like Catherine, who came later. Indeed, there was no more direct route to sainthood than martyrdom.

Catherine practically craved maltreatment—the harsher the better—as she believed her suffering was the one true way to pay for her sins and the sins of others. She celebrated this three-year period in her life, when she was so utterly alone, in a letter to a Sienese nun, "First you find your cell, and you see that inside is a bed. It is clear that you need your cell, but your cell isn't all that you need. No, you turn your glance and your longing to the bed, where you'll find your rest. And this is what you have to do: go into the dwelling, the cell of self-knowledge. There I want you to open the eyes of your understanding, with loving desire. Walk across the cell and get into bed, the bed in which is God's tender goodness, which you find within this cell, yourself. (Surely you can see that your existence has been given you as a favor and not because it was your due.) Notice, daughter, that this bed is covered with a scarlet blanket dyed in the blood of the spotless Lamb. Rest here then, and never leave."

The Dominican friar Tommaso Caffarini wrote of a vision Catherine described to him that happened around 1365, or just after she joined the Mantellate. She saw a magnificent tree loaded with delicious fruit but surrounded by a hedge of prickly thorns, making it hard for anyone to come near. Craving the sweet fruit, people flocked to the tree anyway. After seeing the thorns, though, some resigned themselves to eating only the nearly inedible grain growing nearby. Others managed to maneuver their way through the hedge, but when they saw how high the fruit was, they became discouraged and also went away. But a third group stubbornly fought past the thorns and managed the tough climb up the tree. They alone pushed through the pain and obtained the reward—the fruit. This vision suggested that Catherine was fully aware that, even in the beginning, her road to spiritual fulfillment was destined to be a painful one.

As a member of the Mantellate, she was supposed to revel in mortification of the flesh. Members accepted pain as a form of penance—not in a masochistic way but as a means of melding their own humanity with their Savior's humanity—a humanity that allowed him to suffer on earth. It was a form of worship especially suited for the roles of women of that era. While men were obligated to work, teach and govern, women bore children and produced milk, meaning they were more closely identified with the human form of Christ. Catherine and her contemporaries believed that voluntary suffering was the best way—the only way— to make restitution for the sins of mankind.

And this brings us to Shrove Tuesday in 1367—and back to mystical marriage. Catherine found particular succor in her seclusion on this day, the last night of Carnival in Siena, a time of feasting when revelers partied in the streets with abandon. As Catherine, about 20 at the time, prayed alone in her cell that God might forgive all the sins of the noisy merrymakers, the Virgin Mary and Jesus suddenly appeared to her in a vision, along with King David and St. Dominic. With the music of King David's harp playing in the background, Jesus placed a ring upon Catherine's finger that she believed symbolized their union. According to Raymond, Christ said, "I, your Creator and Savior, espouse you in the faith, that you will keep ever pure until you celebrate your eternal nuptials with me in Heaven. Keep this faith unspotted until you come to me in heaven and celebrate the marriage that has no end. From this time forward, daughter, act firmly and decisively in everything that in my Providence I shall ask you to do. Armed as you are with the strength of faith, you will overcome all your enemies and be happy." The vision of Christ disappeared, but the symbol of the espousal, the ring, was said to be visible to Catherine her entire life, although no one else could see it.

In hagiographers' accounts of her life, Catherine was married with a ring of silver or gold and jewels. But Catherine wrote in many of her letters that we do not marry Christ with gold or silver but with the ring of Christ's foreskin, given during circumcision and accompanied by pain and the shedding of blood. Many women mystics had similar visions, but Catherine's stood apart because it included a wedding ring formed from Christ's own flesh. She saw this flesh less as a substitute for something else and more as evidence of Jesus' blood, shed for the forgiveness of sins. The relic of the Christ child's foreskin was a famous medieval object of reverence—so popular that more than one church laid claim to possessing it in later years.

Tommaso Caffarini recorded another notable event just after the mystical marriage. "While she was in her room praying and intensely desiring Jesus' friendship, it was as if she was repeating, 'Kiss me with a kiss of your mouth,' and the Lord appeared to her and gave her a kiss with which she was exceedingly delighted." Those words, "kiss me with a kiss of your mouth," have been the epitome of the spiritual life to many generations of mystics. As Bynum wrote, "The humanity of Christ, understood as including his full participation in bodiliness, was a central and characteristic theme in the religiosity of late medieval women. Often it had erotic or sensual overtones."

After the mystical marriage, Raymond referred to Catherine as "spouse of the Lord . . . called on by him to bear children to him in the spirit." To Catherine, her mystical marriage helped her prepare for even greater service to God and neighbor. As Giacinto D'Urso, an expert on Catherine's mysticism, put it, "The divine Spouse had not given her the ring of mystical union so that she could enjoy by herself the celestial joys; because she was united to Him, she would also then have to go out of the little paradise of her retreat to pour out on others the richness of her graces."

And so, after her spiritual union with Jesus was complete, Catherine's retreat from the world—and the blissful solitude of her cell—also came to an abrupt end. She grudgingly rejoined her family at dinnertime (although she still refused to eat) after Jesus asked her to in a vision. She initially balked at the request, wondering why she should sit and go through the motions with the family when Christ was all the nourishment her body and soul needed. She even challenged Jesus by quoting scripture back to him, saying, "One does not live by bread alone." But Jesus insisted that it was time for her to go out into the world and to mingle with the masses, no matter how much she had enjoyed basking in the solitude of her cell, her refuge. She would spend her entire life exploring the repercussions of her mystical marriage, but one thing was clear: it was time to venture forth, time to secure peace in the church, time to bring people together. She had eyes only for her groom, but she would be alone with her beloved Christ no more.

FOUR

Just What the Times Needed

In the fourteenth century, Catherine's public persona as a strong-willed woman who never backed down was extraordinary to the point of being freakish. At the time, women were so subservient to men that they didn't speak unless spoken to. And when they were spoken to, they kept their eyes lowered. Legally, women were not allowed to appear in court. They weren't allowed to hold any public, political or professional office or to become a member of any of Italy's influential guilds, such as the dyers' guild Catherine's father belonged to. And they weren't allowed to wear anything that was not of their husband's choosing. Women without brothers were able to inherit land from their fathers, but they were forced to surrender it to their husbands as soon as they married. Always, the law excluded women as second-class citizens. "The good woman was invisible. She wasn't supposed to leave the house. She wasn't even supposed to be seen standing at the window of the house," said Elizabeth Petroff, a professor of comparative literature at the University of Massachusetts, Amherst. "Yes, people looked askance [at Catherine], but she won them over, many times. She must have been just what the times needed."

While in the public eye, Catherine was surrounded by a growing army of disciples who doggedly trailed her through the streets of Siena. The group included her adored sister-in-law Lisa Colombini, whose husband was Catherine's brother Bartolomeo, a woman Catherine called "my sister-in-law according to the flesh, but my sister in Christ." Catherine's own sister Lisa also followed her, as did many young Dominican friars. Members of the group were nearly inseparable, attending Mass together once or twice a day and confession at least once a week. So great was the affection of these followers that they began to call her "Mamma," as Pope Benedict XVI reminded an audience in 2010. He said they did so because, as her children, they looked to her for spiritual nourishment. He said, "Today, too, the Church receives great benefit from the exercise of spiritual motherhood by so many women, lay and consecrated, who nourish souls with thoughts of God, who strengthen the people's faith and direct Christian life towards ever loftier peaks. 'Son, I say to you and call you', Catherine wrote to one of her spiritual sons, Giovanni Sabbatini, 'inasmuch as I give birth to you in continuous prayers and desire in the presence of God, just as a mother gives birth to a son.'"

As she went forth into the world, away from her cell, Catherine wasn't afraid to speak her mind or lecture even the most powerful of men if she thought they would benefit from it. But before taking on her new role, she experienced two tragic episodes in 1368, when she was 21. First, the health of her beloved father deteriorated rapidly during this period. We're not sure what might have been wrong with Giacomo, only that he suddenly took to his bed, quite ill. Catherine stayed glued to his side, certain the end was near, praying for his soul. According to Raymond's account, she begged God to show mercy on her father so that he might not suffer in purgatory. God apparently argued against the idea—although it's not clear why—but Catherine negotiated a plea bargain by imploring God to permit her to suffer any punishments due her father in his place. A severe pain then shot like lightning into Catherine's side before wandering all over her body, and she was barely able to move. She later revealed that remnants of this pain stayed with her the rest of her life. And yet she accepted it not with resentment, but with gratitude, telling her father that he was now free to die in peace. Giacomo passed away on August 22, at which point Catherine became the primary caregiver for her mother, Lapa, who by then was around 60.

The momentous year 1368 also saw the complete collapse of Siena's government and a subsequent wave of riots, revolts and slaughter. Between September 1368 and January 1369, no less than six governments were toppled and supplanted. The city of Florence tried to step in and arbitrate an end to the chaos, but to no avail.

Catherine couldn't help but become drawn into the quagmire. In the years following the plague, her family had shown a keener interest in city politics and how they impact the economy. Being dyers, they belonged to a coalition of tradesmen that supported the ruling faction of twelve people from the citizens' party known as "le Dodici." This is the group that had seized power in 1355. More than a decade later, though, the nobles began turning against the Dodici, and, on September 2, 1368, a group of them broke into the Palazzo Pubblico, the imposing Gothic town hall building on the south side of the Piazza del Campo, and threw out the sitting twelve.

The nobles quickly ushered in a new government—the Government of Nine—that lasted all of three weeks. On September 24, members of the powerful Salimbeni family—made up of wealthy tax collectors—rushed fully armed out into the streets. There they joined members from the old party of the Dodici and threw open the city gates to soldiers of the Holy Roman Empire. The tenacious group fought its way, alleyway by alleyway, to the front door of the Palazzo Pubblico, and the building was taken over yet again. They then set up a new Government of Twelve, Difensori del Popolo Sienese, or the defenders of the people. After only a few weeks of relative calm, they, too, were ousted. This time, fifteen Defenders, or Reformers as they called themselves, stood at the helm. In the months that followed, more battles raged, between all sorts of factions, and Catherine's hometown was racked with revolution and anarchy. It wasn't until the following summer that some semblance of peace was restored. The banished nobles returned, joining forces with yet another group of fifteen Reformers, and they somehow managed to hold the reins until 1385. But sparring among the various parties—and among the families of vengeful men loyal to these parties—went on in spite of the relatively stable government. This constant unrest kept everyone in the city on edge—and the hospitals packed with the wounded.

Despite her family's involvement in local politics, Catherine's unwavering belief in a universal common good that recognizes the worthiness and voices of all people—no matter what their background, affiliation or social status—made her a powerful advocate for peace. The outspoken young woman had, through her confident and heartfelt oratory, become quite adept at calming troubled waters—able to persuade the haughtiest of nobles and the most pompous of citizens to take a more passive, conciliatory approach. Although Giacomo had been spared the sight of wanton violence, Catherine and the rest of the family were in the thick of it, unable to avoid the clash of weapons that so often erupted right outside their doorsteps. According to nineteenth-century biographer Josephine Butler, who wrote *Life of St. Catherine of Siena*, "All that Catherine saw and heard contributed to encourage in the young girl the strong republican love of liberty, and to confirm in her the conviction that human life is no holiday pastime, but a prolonged struggle between opposing elements, for nations as well as for the individual."

Biographers' accounts begin casting Catherine in the role of peacemaker around the age of 21. During the fighting in Siena in 1368, Catherine was said to have mediated many times between the various factions. Although details are few, some historical accounts have cited a speech she gave in the streets around this time that reportedly drew more than 2,000 people. In it, she beseeched the people to stop fighting. Although she remained outside partisan politics, Catherine would have sounded off against murderous reprisals. She crossed many, though, by refusing to turn her back on any faction, not even on the power-hungry Salimbeni family, longtime enemies of the downtrodden.

Helping to shape Catherine's public image during this time— an image that was recast significantly in the years just after her three-year stint of solitude in her cell—was her continuation of her extreme fasting.

Indeed, Catherine's general abstinence from food proved to be one of the saint's most enduring—and most analyzed—practices. Although other holy women living many centuries ago also controlled their eating, Catherine's asceticism was in a category all its own. Growing up, she had never eaten much, and by the age of 20, she plunged full-force into a lifestyle of self-denial. When she forced herself to swallow something, usually under the watchful eye of a worried Lapa, she shoved twigs down her throat afterward to induce vomiting.

Skeptics, including many who were quite religious themselves, pounced. Some called her a fraud and accused her of eating in secret. Others said her inability to eat was the handiwork of the devil. Still others went so far as to call her overall character into question, presuming her to be immoral and arrogant. Raymond wrote how "she could hardly exercise an act of devotion in public without suffering criticisms, impediments and persecutions, particularly from those who ought to have protected and encouraged her in those very actions."

When it came to eating, though, Raymond verified with his own eyes how much agony trying to digest even small amounts of food wrought on Catherine.

> Although she used neither meat, nor wine, nor drink, nor eggs, and did not even touch bread, what she took, or rather, what she tried to take, caused her such sufferings that those who saw her, however hard-hearted they were, were moved to compassion; her stomach could digest nothing, and rejected whatever was taken into it; she afterwards suffered the most terrible pains and her whole body appeared to be swollen; she did not swallow the herbs which she chewed, she only drew from them their juice and rejected their substance. She then took pure water to cool her mouth; but every day she was forced to throw up what she had taken, and that with so much difficulty that it was necessary to assist her by every possible means. As I was frequently witness of this suffering, I felt an extreme compassion for her, and I counseled her to let men talk, and spare herself such torture.

Catherine's eating issues served a higher purpose, however. "Asceticism" comes from the Greek word *askesis*, meaning "exercise, training, practice"; ascetics renounce worldly pleasures that detract from spiritual enlightenment. In Christianity, it's common to connect an indulgence of the flesh with a weakness of the mind, and so by denying earthly comforts—even eating—adherents are able to reach a higher spiritual plane. In Catherine's time, ritualistic fasting was employed as a means of preventing gluttony—a sin that was ascribed an enormous destructive power by the Bible—while having the added benefit of helping atone for past sins.

Professors Mario Reda and Giuseppe Sacco at the University of Siena argue that, for Catherine, yielding to food was the most egregious failure possible. "To yield to food was to yield to sin, to deceive God, to lose all the power that she had laboriously garnered, erasing the sense of identity gained from the victory over her opposition to family regulation," they say. "It is of little matter, then, if she did not feel understood by her opponents (in that time compared to ours). Indeed, incomprehension provided the stimulus to go on. The challenge continued to provide a way for her to confirm her true sense of identity."

To Caroline Walker Bynum and other historians, Catherine's extreme fasting was also a means of manipulating her male-dominated environment so that she—a mere woman—could live as full a life of Christian piety as possible. If the medieval church had not been so misogynistic, they charged, Catherine might have enjoyed a legitimate role in the church and might not have had to starve herself to feel closer to God.

Catherine herself, in a 1373 letter, attributed her extreme fasting to "God, who by a most singular mercy, allowed me to correct the vice of gluttony." Raymond once asked her whether she didn't at least sometimes experience the sensation of hunger. "God satisfied me so in the Holy Eucharist that it is impossible for me to desire any species of corporal nourishment," she replied. "His sole presence satiates me, and I acknowledge that, to be happy, it even suffices for me to see a priest who has just said Mass." According to Raymond, she could sense the mere presence of a priest who had touched the Sacrament, and it would console her to such a degree that any and all food became superfluous.

Despite her strong spirit, though, there were days when Catherine's body was reduced to such a state of feebleness from lack of nutrition that Raymond was worried her legs might no longer support her. Thankfully, those moments were fleeting. "As soon as any opportunity arose to honor the Divine Name, or do good to some soul, there would be a sudden wonderful change, and without the help of any medicine Catherine would regain all her life and strength and be strong and cheerful," Raymond wrote. "She would get up, walk about, and go about her work as easily as the people who were with her and who were in good health; she did not know the meaning of fatigue." He challenged his readers: "Where did all this come from, if not from the Spirit who delights in such works? What could not be done by nature, He did by miracle. Is it not perfectly clear that it was He who gave strength to her soul and body?"

Interestingly enough, Catherine never glorified her fasting or held it up as an example that others should emulate. Instead, she urged her followers to abstain only moderately—or not at all. If anything, she bent over backward to make sure those around her ate regularly, even as she denied herself. In 1374, famine forced those in Siena to use old moldy flour to make bread that left a horrible taste in people's mouths. When fresh flour finally did come to market, Catherine's close friend, a widow named Alessia Saracini, told her that she planned to throw out the bad flour and bake only with the good. Catherine immediately balked, citing all the needy people who still needed to be fed. She vowed to bake the flour into bread herself no matter how old it was, and to distribute it around town. And she did just that. Those who ate her bread marveled at its flavor, saying they'd never tasted anything so delicious. Not only that, but the supply of old flour never diminished even though countless loaves were created from it. When Raymond heard about the miracle, he asked Catherine how she was able to do it. She told him that the Virgin Mary had offered her help in a vision. Working together, the number of loaves just kept multiplying. "No wonder," Raymond wrote, "that that bread seemed so sweet, since it was made by the perfect hands of the holy queen, in whose most sacred body, the Trinity made the bread that came down from heaven to give life to all unbelievers."

Another time, around 1374 or 1375, a Florentine priest who had gotten word of Catherine's fasts wrote to her, warning that the devil could be using her inability to eat to lead her astray. Catherine politely thanked him for his concern but told him not to concern himself with her fasting. She said she was forever vigilant because of her own weakness and the devil's ingenuity. Always clever at answering her male critics, she told him:

> You wrote especially that I ask God for the ability to eat. I tell you father—and I say it in the sight of God—that in every way I have been able to manage I have forced myself to take food once or twice a day. Over and over I have prayed and do pray and will continue to pray to God for the grace to live as other people do in this matter of eating—if it is his will, for it certainly is mine. When I have done as much as I can, I enter within myself to get to know my own weakness and God, and I realize that he has given me a very special grace to overcome the vice of gluttony. But I tell you, it very often makes me sad that I have not overcome it simply for love. I for my part don't know what else to do about it, except to beg you to ask supreme eternal Truth to grant me the grace of being able to eat—if it pleases him and is for his greater honor

and my soul's good. And I'm sure that God's goodness will not make light of your prayers.

Later, Catherine elaborated even further. Penance, she wrote, should be considered the key to being virtuous, a goal that can take a lifetime to achieve: "No one should judge that he has greater perfection because he performs great penances and gives himself in excess to the staying of the body than he who does less, inasmuch as neither virtue nor merit consists therein; for otherwise he would be an evil case, who for some legitimate reason was unable to do actual penance. Merit consists in the virtue of love alone, flavored with the light of true discretion, without which the soul is worth nothing."

Maybe Catherine had wanted to eat—at least in the beginning. But her inability to do so became a compulsion she no longer cared to cure, and the self-denial only became more severe as time went on.

In his 1985 book *Holy Anorexia,* history professor Rudolph M. Bell argued compellingly that although Catherine and other medieval mystics fit the classic profile of a modern anorexic, what they experienced was really something very different—a condition he labeled "holy anorexia." Holy anorexics (the condition also has been referred to as *anorexia mirabilis,* which literally means a "miraculous loss of appetite") strive not to be thin but to be spiritually pure. Women suffering from anorexia nervosa share an intense dread of gaining weight while holy anorexics dread being sinful. Bell conceded that the two forms are "psychologically analogous" across the centuries, but said the rationale among those afflicted in Catherine's time and modern anorexics is distinct. Although in both cases, the anorexics are perfectionistic, Catherine and other saints deprived their bodies in a single-mindedness to be joined with God. A complete renunciation of the body was the one way in which women could convincingly affirm their godliness to those around them. St. Margaret of Cortona, who lived in the thirteenth century, fasted while tending to the needy of her home city. "I want to die of starvation in order to satiate the poor," she wrote.

The period of holy anorexia was, however, not to last. Already in the sixteenth century the church was beginning to frown on such extreme asceticism, and those who did without food began to be labeled as witches who should be consigned to the stake. Indeed, after the Middle Ages, men regained control over women's bodies by charging the numerous "fasting saints" with witchcraft under the Inquisition. In some places, women could prove they were not witches only if they weighed a sufficient amount on government-designated scales. Again, the relationship between self-starvation and religion was particularly pronounced for women. Even Catherine was occasionally accused of being a witch, to the point that she would have to ostentatiously pretend to eat something to placate her critics.

Despite all this, Catherine kept busy, living her love for Christ passionately and energetically. She began dabbling more in Italian politics as well as in broader European conflicts. She dictated the first of her approximately 385 letters around 1370 or 1371, when she was 23 or 24 years old. She began taking corrupt church leaders to task and telling them the pope had no business being anywhere but in Rome. Then, on December 19, 1370, when Catherine was 23, Pope Urban V passed away in Avignon. Only three years earlier, in the fall of 1367, Urban had returned to Rome, albeit briefly, the first pope to do so since 1304. He had hoped that, by being there, he'd be better able to rebuild his rocky relationship with the papal states in Italy. But after seeing little progress on that front (and missing the pleasures of Avignon), he gave up and went back to France in September 1370. But before he left Rome, the Virgin Mary appeared to St. Bridget of Sweden in a dream and warned that the pope would die if he were allowed to leave. Bridget had the gift of prophecy and served as a valuable adviser to the pope. Agreeing with Catherine that the papacy should be based in Rome, she relayed the warning to Urban V, and, sure enough, he was dead of unspecified causes only three months later. After that, another Frenchman, Pierre Roger de Beaufort, was elected pope and took the name Gregory XI. The unruly Romans grew more rebellious and the turmoil continued.

Meanwhile, within Catherine's biological family, Giacomo's death had left Catherine and the other members of the Benincasa household badly shaken. Financial troubles became more of a headache, although it's not clear why money was such an issue. Politics may have been to blame. Although Catherine stayed above the political fray, her two eldest brothers, Bartolomeo and Stefano, had aligned themselves with the Dodici. And, like most other members of this party, the Benincasa family apparently fared poorly after the change in government. At one point, the atmosphere was so toxic that Bartolomeo and Stefano came under attack, chased down by an angry mob hell-bent on seeing them dead or run out of town. Details of the incident are recorded in *Miracoli of St. Catherine*, written by an anonymous resident of Siena around 1374. It describes throngs of rioters combing the streets of Siena in search of the brothers. The pair first holed up in the family home but soon realized that was the last place they should be. A friend then recommended that they take shelter in a nearby church, but Catherine insisted that the hospital of Santa Maria della Scala, where she had often prayed with patients, posed less of a risk. However, getting there required the brothers to pass through the center of town—precisely where rioters were look-ing for them. Clad in her white veil and black cape, a determined Catherine acted as their escort. And it worked. No one made any attempt to approach them. Instead, people dropped their weapons and actually bowed to Catherine as they walked by, as if she were royalty. Although her religious habit provided some security, it was her personal reputation more than anything else that acted as a shield, protecting her and her brothers from the crowd's wrath.

The loss of Giacomo, money troubles and ongoing political turmoil were gnawing away at Lapa's strength, and soon the old woman's health began to falter. Catherine loved her mother and prayed morning and night that she be allowed to live, especially as she knew her mother had not yet completely given her whole self and mind to God. Lapa's condition nevertheless grew worse, and one day she died—at least that's how it looked to everyone at her bedside. Catherine cried out, "Oh my dear Lord, is this how You keep the promise You once made me that none in this house should suffer eternal death? You promised me too that You would not take my mother from this world before she could leave it in a state of grace, and here she lies dead, without having confessed or received the Sacrament. My beloved Savior, I call to You in Your great mercy, do not fail me! I will not go alive from Your feet until You give me my mother back."

After Catherine's speech, the women around the deathbed looked on as life began to seep back into Lapa's body. The rosi-ness returned to her cheeks. She breathed faintly and moved her arms and legs. A day or two later, Lapa declared herself better, and soon she was her old cantankerous self again. According to Raymond, the women who witnessed this miracle included Lisa, Lapa's daughter-in-law, a member of the Mantellate who spent time on a regular basis with Catherine and her friends. A strong woman, Lapa ended up outliving her daughters and most of her grandchildren in a tiny house near the Porta Romana, far from the home she had run with Giacomo as a busy housewife bringing up her large and happy brood. Later in life, she sometimes complained, "I think God has wedged my soul crossways in my body so that it cannot come out."

Catherine shouldered many of the burdens where her aging mother was concerned. Once, she even chastised her oldest brother Stefano after he had moved to Florence to start a new business for shirking his duties when it came to Lapa. She wrote as any typical angry sister might to an irresponsible brother:

> And I would not have it escape your mind that you should correct you of your ingratitude, and your ignoring of the duty you owe your mother, to which you are held by the commandment of God. I have seen your ingratitude multiply so that you have not even paid her the due of help that you owe: to be sure, I have an excuse for you in this, because you could not; but if you had been able, I do not know that you would have done it, since you have left her in scarcity even of words. Oh, ingratitude! Have you not considered the sorrow of her labor, nor the milk that she drew from her breast, nor the many troubles that she has had, over you and all the others? And should you say to me that she has had no compassion on us, I saw that it is not so; for she has had so much on you and the others that it cost her dear. But suppose it was true—you are under obligation to her, not she to you. She did not take her flesh from you, but gave you hers. I beg you to correct this fault and others, and to pardon my ignorance. For did I not love your soul, I would not say to you what I do.

The death of her father, coupled with the deteriorating health of her mother, must have taken a toll. Even though Catherine had been pulling away from her birth family connections while embracing more closely a new family of friends and followers, she still held her mother and siblings in great affection.

During the turbulent months of the summer of 1370, Catherine experienced a bombardment of powerful visions that, she said, made clear to her the secret mysteries of faith. "To explain in our defective language what I saw," she said years later, "would seem to me like blaspheming the Lord or dishonoring him by my speech. Great is the distance between what the intellect apprehends, rapt and illumined and strengthened by God, and what can be expressed with words. They seem almost contradictory." Once, as she prayed fervently for a purer heart, she felt a flood of blood and fire wash over her in what was later described as a mystical cleansing of her body and soul. A day or two later, she experienced another bizarre episode that she referred to as an "exchange of hearts" with Christ. Raymond wrote that Jesus came to Catherine and appeared to open her left side so that he could take out her heart. Later, Christ returned again to Catherine, carrying a bright red human heart in his hands. This time he opened her chest and placed the heart inside her. He said: "Dearest daughter, as the other day I took your heart that you offered to me, behold now I give you mine, and henceforth it will be in the place that yours occupied." Afterward, when trying to describe the event, Catherine said, "Don't you see that I am no longer who I was, but that I am changed into another person?"

Then, on a Sunday in the fall of 1370, Catherine died. Or at least that's the way it appeared to those attending to her in a scene eerily reminiscent of that involving her mother only a few months earlier. Catherine had fallen into a trance lasting longer than most—more than four hours—with her sister-in-law, Lisa, standing watch. So convinced was Lisa that the end was near that she sent for Tommaso to administer last rites. Upon arrival, he watched as Catherine took what appeared to be her final breath, and then prepared to anoint her body with sacred oils. Four minutes later, though, Catherine started breathing again and soon regained consciousness. Later, she described how the tremendous force of God's love had ripped apart her heart, causing her to temporarily vacate this world. She said, "So great was the fire of divine love and of the desire of uniting myself with him that, if my heart had been made of stone or iron, it would have been broken in the same manner." While she was "dead," Catherine said she had been transported to another dimension where she was given a taste of the afterlife—heaven, hell and purgatory. She also saw images of those who had been her spiritual mentors—the Virgin Mary, St. Dominic and Mary Magdalene, among others. The life-changing event left her reeling with emotion. At first, she was unable to put its impact on her into words, and she did almost nothing for days but cry.

Some time later, though, she was able to explain, quite specifically, the suspension of physical life that had transpired:

While my soul saw all of these things, the eternal Bridegroom said to me, "Do you see the great glory that some are deprived of, and the horrible torments that await them, who offend me? Return, then, and make known to them their errors, their danger, and loss. The salvation of many souls demands your return. No longer will you keep the way of life that you have kept, no longer will you have your cell for a home. You are to leave your own city for the sake and welfare of souls. I will be with you and guide you and bring you back again. I will give you speech and wisdom that no one will be able to withstand. I will lead you before pontiffs and rulers of the churches and all Christian people."

The experience had galvanized her interest in the outside world, and she was about to make an even greater impact with the help of her new family of followers.

FIVE

Fighting Off Threats

In the fourteenth century, the Christian faith that dominated every aspect of the lives of Catherine and her followers was under threat. Not only from within, as corruption among religious leaders ran rampant. Not only from the sin Catherine saw around her every day and tried so hard to extinguish. But also from forces far away.

For seven centuries, Christianity had been the prevailing religious force across Europe and the Middle East. France, Italy, Spain, Egypt, Syria, Palestine, North Africa and Asia Minor were all Christian territories. But in the seventh century, the Arabs embarked on a conquest of territory in the name of Islam and—within 100 years—Egypt, Spain, Syria, Palestine, North Africa, most of Asia Minor, as well as parts of southern France were taken over. Years of imperial and doctrinal wars had left the region in disarray, making expansion into Christian lands fairly easy. Before long, two-thirds of what had been the Roman Christian world was controlled by Muslims. Islam was on the rise, and the very survival of Christianity was called into question. Or so Catherine and many others thought.

In the Holy Land, a relatively peaceful coexistence between Christians and Muslims had evolved over the previous six centuries. The Arab conquest of Palestine in the seventh century initially had few ramifications for either European Christians making pilgrimages to holy sites or the security of monasteries and Christian communities in the Holy Land. As a result, authorities in Europe paid almost no heed—at least initially—to the political and religious affairs of such distant places.

The turning point came in 1009, when Al-Hakim bi-Amr Allah, a Fatimid caliph (part of a dynasty named after the Prophet Muhammad's daughter Fatimah) in Cairo known for his erratic behavior, ordered that the churches and synagogues of Palestine, Egypt and Syria be destroyed. With an eye toward uniting the Islamic world under his aegis, the fanatical leader even set eradicative hordes loose on the holiest Christian site in the world—the Church of the Holy Sepulchre, also known as the Church of the Resurrection, in Old Jerusalem. Christians everywhere were outraged. Over the next several years, he reversed all policies of tolerance toward Christians and Jews while vigorously promoting a belief in his own divinity. But then one night in February 1021, Al-Hakim—one of history's most controversial figures—apparently rode out of the southern gates of Cairo on a donkey, as he often did, only this time never to be seen or heard from again. Speculations and rumors of assassination—or the individual decision to abandon the demands of royal life—swirled, but none were ever verified. The only thing known for sure is that Al-Hakim's body was never found, but his legacy lives on. For some, he was an infallible descendant of the Prophet Muhammad. For others, he was a persecutor who tried to destroy a way of life. But Al-Hakim also built libraries and hospitals, and his many followers founded the Druze sect near Cairo. Meanwhile, by 1049, with the blessing of the caliph's successor, the Byzantine Christians had been allowed to rebuild the Church of the Holy Sepulchre on a modest scale. But the issue ran deeper than mere bricks and mortar. A seed had been planted, and stories began to circulate in the West about the continuous Muslim harassment of peaceful Christian pilgrims traveling to Jerusalem.

One of the greatest and most enduring empires of all time, the Byzantine Empire's roots can be traced to AD 330, when the Roman emperor Constantine I dedicated a "New Rome" capital on the site of the ancient Greek colony of Byzantium (later Constantinople, now Istanbul). Christian in faith, the Byzantines were perennially at war with the Muslims. Indeed, many historians argue that without Byzantium as a bulwark, Europe would have been completely overpowered by waves of Islamic invaders. As pilgrimages became increasingly dangerous, Christians began banding together and brandishing weapons to protect themselves as they made the long trek across the deserts to Christianity's holiest sites. Desperate, the Byzantines appealed for help, directing their requests squarely at the person they saw as the chief Western authority: the pope, who was only too happy to help coordinate Christian resistance to Muslim attacks.

In 1094, Pope Urban II called on all available warriors to journey to the area now commonly referred to as the Middle East in order to reclaim the Holy Land. It was one of the first volleys in a series of wars that would come to be known as the Crusades, conflicts that would continue for centuries and reverberate into the modern era. In return, Urban's holy warriors would be exempted from taxes and also would be granted an unprecedented spiritual reward—the absolution of all sins. It was to be a free pass to an escape from the torments of hell, which is where they most certainly were headed following their lives of sin and violence. Urban was unequivocal in his exhortations for support.

"A horrible tale has gone forth. An accursed race utterly alienated from God . . . has invaded the lands of the Christians and
depopulated them by the sword, plundering, and fire," he said, in
what was one of the most influential speeches of the Middle Ages.
"Tear that land from the wicked race and subject it to yourselves."

The rallying cry worked its intended magic. Crowds of angry Christians began gathering and shouting *"Deus vult! Deus vult!"*
("God wills it!") to the point that Urban made *"Deus vult"* the
battle cry of the First Crusade. He had successfully united Christian Europe, and, all told, between 60,000 and 100,000 people
responded to his call to march on Jerusalem, not only for religious reasons, but also in search of riches and adventure. For a
time, it seemed as though all of Europe was heading east, ready to
seek revenge on those who attacked Christianity. When the first
crusaders took control of Jerusalem in July 1099, they butchered
some 30,000 of the city's Jewish and Muslim inhabitants in a
two-day bloodbath. (Pope Urban II died on June 29 before hearing the news.) At first Europeans were shocked by the enormity
of the massacre, but they changed their tune once scholars started
characterizing Muslims as a savage race. From an Islamic point of
view, the Crusades were barbaric and unwarranted onslaughts lev-
eled by cruel and relentless European Christians. From a Christian
point of view, the Crusades were the only way to wrest the Holy
Land from Muslim control. No doubt the Crusades were a starting point of a millennium-long bitter hostility between the Arabs
and the West, a clash that inflicted lasting psychological scars.

The Crusades continued on and off for centuries. In 1371, just
months after his election, Pope Gregory XI—a theologian with a
keen interest in international politics—announced his intention
to launch a new crusade aimed at halting Turkish advances in the
Adriatic, an idea that Catherine and others bent on the destruction

of Muslims as a political and military force immediately rallied around. (The saintly young woman who abhorred violence at home seemed to have no qualms about incurring bloodshed in distant lands.)

In early dictated letters to cardinals and other church leaders, Catherine extolled the spiritual benefits of war waged on behalf of God and the Holy Land. The pope, too, urged Christians to make peace among themselves so that they could better channel all their energies into fighting the Turks. Working together, Catherine and Gregory encountered few dissenters save for one—Bridget of Sweden, who died in 1373. The papal adviser generally supported Gregory, but in this instance she sounded an apocalyptic alarm against the crusade. From her point of view, the forays were a reckless way of providing the pope with a convenient cover for neglecting more pressing matters at home. She also believed they gave bloodthirsty soldiers free rein to plunder and pillage on a more extensive scale than they could in Europe.

Catherine saw things differently. She considered the Islamic warriors a threat to all of Christianity and the proposed crusade as the only way to bring together a fragmented Christendom. Throughout her lifetime, she reported seeing many visions of crowds of martyrs willing to give their lives in order to preserve the Holy Land. They were warriors who had previously fought only for their own personal gain but who were now joining forces for the good of their religion. Many in this era who later became saints were involved in promoting the plan, not out of bloodthirsty greed, but because they believed Islam was a nefarious menace that had to be stopped.

So zealous a promoter of a new crusade was Catherine that she even tried to recruit the help of an infamous English mercenary, Sir John Hawkwood, who had plundered his way through

Italy. In a letter written in either 1371 or 1372 to the professional soldier famous for his handling of infantry, Catherine said that her "soul desires now to see you quite changed, and enrolled under the Cross of Christ crucified; you and all your comrades forming a Company of Christ, and marching against the infidels who possess the holy places where the Sweet and Eternal Truth lived and died for us. I beg of you, therefore, in His name, that since God and our Holy Father give the orders to march against the infidels, and since you are so fond of fighting and making war, you will fight no more against Christians, for that offends God, but go and fight against their enemies." Hawkwood initially promised to support the crusade, but he never followed through. Today, Catherine's history with Hawkwood is celebrated in a painting that hangs at the back of the lovely chapel of the Venerable English College in Rome.

As the pope spoiled for a fight abroad, Europe faced more local problems. From around 1370 to 1374, Italy's once-thriving economy teetered following a series of crop failures and subsequent famines. Catherine did what she could, serving whatever food she could find to the multitudes of hungry residents of Siena. The famine precipitated political crises that made everyone in town suspicious and easily rattled. The people of Siena found themselves in a constant state of paranoia. So sure were they that invaders would show up at any moment, a guard was stationed permanently inside the Piazza del Campo tower. With rumors of possible attacks swirling incessantly, the alarm bells in the tower were nearly always in motion. And with fighting breaking out indiscriminately in the streets, private vigilantes armed to the teeth utilized the houses of Siena's ruling families as impromptu garrisons, ready to counterattack if and when an angry populace came calling.

Throughout the turmoil, Catherine never lost sight of her focus on evangelism. Her overriding goal was always to convert as many sinners as possible, and she cared not a whit about their class, status or history. In a kind but pedantic way, she begged everyone she came upon to repent and be saved—even in the worst of economic and political times. Day after day, she visited and prayed with the sick in their homes and in hospitals, often accompanied by her two close friends and followers, Alessia Saracini—a daughter of one of Siena's most notable families—and Francesca di Clemente Gori—a close disciple and older widow in the Mantellate.

Sometime in the summer or fall of 1369, Catherine actually moved in with Alessia and her family, whose home near the Piazza del Mercato was situated in the very heart of Siena. The location served as a convenient base for a politically active religious woman. Also around this time, Neri di Landoccio Pagliaresi, a Tuscan poet of some renown, joined Catherine's network of laymen and clerics. A bundle of energy, he became one of her favorite and most prolific secretaries. An increasing number of letters went out as he seemed to take dictation at all hours, both day and night. No matter to whom she wrote, the push was for personal conversion. And the language she used was the same no matter whether she was writing to priests, princes or average citizens.

Tommaso, who was still serving as Catherine's confessor and confidant, grew concerned that Catherine was juggling too many responsibilities and that she might inadvertently succumb to temptation unless she got more rest. The remedy, he believed, was a respite, and so he took her outside Siena's walls to visit an Augustinian monastery where the hermit William Flete resided. One of the more unforgettable men of that time, Flete was to have an enormous influence on Catherine's life and development. The Englishman boasted quite the background, having completed his studies to become a master in theology at the University of Cambridge but, for whatever reason, never finishing his degree. Instead, he severed all ties with the English branch of the Augustinians and relocated to Italy, drawn by a movement afoot there to live the Rule of St. Augustine in its original purity. Because of his theological training to become a bachelor of theology, Flete was called *il baccelliere,* or "the bachelor," by his brother monks. He spent his days buried in books, taking breaks only to offer counsel to clergy and anyone else who trekked out from the city to see him. The passage of time has shed no light on the conversation the two shared that day, but we do know it served as the impetus for an important friendship that would last for the rest of Catherine's life.

Flete was probably the first trained theologian Catherine had ever spoken with, an English mystic who thrived on solitude. Through him she became aware of the ideas of St. Augustine of Hippo, the great theologian of the early church who helped formulate the doctrine of original sin. His view of the world helped offset the teachings of Thomas Aquinas that Catherine had absorbed through her Dominican friar friends. Her understanding of the beliefs of both Augustine and Flete gave her the capacity to better refine her own ideas about knowledge of self and knowledge of God. In time, Flete came to appreciate Catherine's many gifts, and, after her death, he wrote an unusually long and flattering sermon describing her many virtues that is still available in the library of Siena. After witnessing her in ecstasy, he wrote about seeing her face transformed into that of an angel or even into that of the Lord.

Not long after meeting Flete, Catherine began telling him what to do—just as she did almost everyone. She urged the Englishman not to allow a penchant for solitude to interfere with what God had planned for him. "I tell you, not only should you say Mass in the convent sometimes during the week when the prior wishes it, but I want you to say it every day, if you see that he wishes it. I want us not to attend only to our own consolations, but we must also care and have compassion for the labors of our neighbors. If you didn't do this it would be a very great fault," she told him. Although Flete did much to make Catherine's work known after her death, he never allowed himself to be absorbed into her inner circle of followers. He was far too happy on the outskirts, cut off from the world in the woods, where he enjoyed hours of uninterrupted prayer and meditation.

As more of Catherine's letters flowed forth, her name became known to an even wider circle of people. Indeed, Catherine became so revered that her presence was requested at a large and important meeting of Dominicans in Florence in early 1374, at which the group's mission and staffing were to be reviewed. Who invited her isn't clear, but it may have been the master of the Dominican order, Elias Raymond, a highly respected French friar of Toulouse. It was at this meeting that Catherine was first introduced to a well-regarded priest named Raymond of Capua. A man of tremendous intellect, Raymond was handpicked by Elias to be Catherine's new confessor. Seventeen years her senior, he was a more appropriate pick than Tommaso for someone like Catherine, whose reputation was drawing large crowds everywhere she went. Of the day they met, Catherine said later that she had heard a voice while watching Raymond at the altar. It said, "This is my beloved servant. This is he to whom I will entrust you." Catherine was overjoyed to be matched up with him.

Born in Capua, Italy, in 1330, Raymond was a descendant of the city's noblest family. Besides being Catherine's adviser, he would go on to become a leading member of the Dominican order and its master general from 1380 until his death in 1399. He was beatified in 1899 and is still revered by Catholics around the world. He was an eyewitness to much of Catherine's adult life and his hagiography is invaluable. In Raymond, Catherine found her most sympathetic friend. Among other things, Raymond showed a greater understanding of her constant need to receive Communion, which Tommaso, for some reason, had not indulged. Raymond was more willing to give in to her desires.

But being a cautious man, Raymond was at first less than enthusiastic about his appointment as Catherine's confessor and confidant. At the time, he was teaching at a Dominican church in Florence, a job he enjoyed and found greatly rewarding. And Catherine was a stranger, even if her reputation for holiness preceded her. But his hesitancy was short-lived, especially after their first full day together. "She kept on speaking on the subject she had begun. And as she spoke my sins came before my mind with a clarity I had never before experienced," he wrote. "The veil was torn from my eyes, and I saw myself standing at the bar of my Divine Judge . . . I burst out into such a torrent of tears and sobs as, I must reluctantly confess, made me fear my very breast and heart would be ruptured. Catherine discreetly said not another word, as though this was the very purpose for which she had come."

Aside from Raymond, while in Florence, she also befriended Niccolo Soderini, a wealthy Florentine merchant who would become a trusted adviser on Florentine affairs, and she became acquainted with a rich man named Piero Canigiani, who would help bankroll a later visit by Catherine and her followers.

When it came to Raymond, he and Catherine cemented their partnership in 1374 when they returned together to Siena, only to be met by tragedy. Indeed, when they arrived at the gates of her city, they were aghast at the sight of carts filled with the dead. The Black Death that had first decimated the city in the year of Catherine's birth had struck again. She was now 27 and about to witness another especially dismal year for Siena and all of Italy. It seemed that oil, meat, bread and almost everything else were in short supply. The situation was so dire that the local governments took control of bread production, doling out loaves through a lottery system. Even then, there was never enough to go around. Working intimately alongside Catherine day in and day out during this time of crisis helped build Raymond's confidence in the holy woman's prowess. He watched as Catherine and her followers labored selflessly to care for the sick and the dead, which eventually numbered in the many thousands. Since there were no medicines to be administered, Catherine mainly would have been responsible for cleaning patients or performing other tasks no one else had the stomach to do. In a scene reminiscent of the plague of 1348, bodies started gathering in the streets and stayed there until someone scooped them up to be buried in the great trenches dug just outside town. When those filled up, more trenches were created farther afield. Among the dead were one of Catherine's sisters, two of her brothers and at least seven nieces and nephews. She dug each of their graves with her own hands. While just about everyone who was able to flee did so, Catherine and her followers refused to budge, going from hospital to hospital and from home to home to pray over the sick and to prepare the bodies of the dead for burial. Day and night she moved fearlessly among the infected, although she apparently carried a smelling bottle that was designed to act as a deterrent against the pestilential air.

Catherine is credited with many miraculous cures—or cures that at least appeared miraculous—during this time, including one involving Matteo di Ceni de Fazzio, rector of the hospital Casa della Misericordia, an important center in the fight against the plague. Matteo sent for Raymond to make his last confession, but when Catherine heard the news, she rushed to his bedside, well aware of the huge role he played at the hospital. "Rise up at once, Meser Matteo!" she cried. "This is not the time to be lying in bed." And with that, the man who had looked like he was dying only minutes before got up, strong and robust, and went straight back to his work in the hospital. Her prayers also saved Raymond when he too came perilously close to death after succumbing to the plague. Praying over him, she begged God to make him well, and, in a short time, the color returned to his cheeks and he was perfectly fine again. "Go now," she told him, "and work for the salvation of souls, and give thanks to Almighty God, who had preserved your life."

Catherine cemented her reputation as an extraordinary holy woman by both her exertions among the stricken population and the steadfastness of her faith. "Never did she appear more admirable than at this time," wrote a priest who had known her from girlhood. "She was always with the plague-stricken: she prepared them for death and buried them with her own hands. I myself witnessed the joy with which she nursed them and the wonderful efficacy of her words, which brought about many conversions."

She also came to the aid of plague victims outside Siena. She and Raymond and a few other disciples traveled mostly by foot to a little town called Varazze, about 19 miles west of Genoa, that had seen its population very nearly wiped out by the plague. Varazze was well known as the birthplace of Jacopo de Voragine, author of *The Golden Legend*, an extremely popular book in the Middle Ages. Catherine told a handful of citizens who had survived the epidemic that if they built a chapel in his honor, their town would be exempt from the plague. They followed her instructions and constructed the chapel, and the plague never again returned to Varazze.

Around this time, in 1374, Catherine also dictated a letter to her mother, who always worried about her when she was on the road. She told Lapa that she longed to see her be the kind of mother who was concerned not only about her body, but also about her soul. "I think that if you loved my soul more than my body all exaggerated tenderness in you would die, and you would not suffer so much when you lack my presence in the flesh. You would find consolation, and you would be able to bear the sorrow I cause you for the glory of God, when you thought that I was seeking grace and strength for my soul in working for the glory of God," she wrote. She reminded Lapa of the courage of the Virgin Mary, who selflessly stood by as her beloved son was put to death on the cross: "I know that you wish me to obey the will of God. It was His will that I should go, my absence was ordained by the secret plans of Providence, and has not been without the most valuable results," she said.

But just as her mother feared, Catherine eventually fell victim to the deadly scourge. This time it was a worried Raymond who was praying over her. He watched her face, burning up with fever, transform into the face of a man whom he took to be the suffering Christ. Raymond trembled, not sure what he should do for the pious woman put in his charge. As always, Catherine prayed to be a martyr. But then the Virgin Mary came to her in some kind of dream, showing Catherine all the souls that would be united with God if only Catherine lived on and helped them. And so Catherine survived and recovered.

Caring for the sick is a current that runs through Catherine's life—not just during times of plague. Indeed, one of the most notable—and revolting—stories surrounding Catherine's adult life involves her caring for the sick. Around 1373, when Catherine was 26, she volunteered to care for a disagreeable woman named Andrea, who had a cancerous wound on her breast that was apparently so foul-smelling no one else dared go near her. According to Raymond, "when Catherine heard this she realized that this invalid, abandoned by practically everyone else, was being assigned specially to herself by God. At once she went to the house, approached the sufferer with a friendly smile, and cheerfully offered herself as her nurse, to attend her as long as her sickness would last." The saint tried to show no sign of aversion as she attended her patient. But one day, as she washed the wound, Catherine's body betrayed her, and she couldn't stop herself from throwing up. Angry at her own deficiencies, she decided to do something drastic to demonstrate her great love of her neighbor. And so she "bent over the sick woman and pressed her mouth and nose upon the festering sore, and in that posture she remained a long time, until she felt that the power of the Spirit had subdued the nausea of the flesh, and that she had stamped out the rebellion of the flesh against the spirit."

Later, when she again became nauseous while changing Andrea's bandages, she apparently heard a voice that said, "What great pride you have there; you are not ashamed to detest Christ in your neighbor." Raymond recorded what happened next: "Fresh from her recent conquests in the power of the Holy Spirit, and strong in the heroic virtues (the Lord) had brought her, she could not bear that her body should again rebel against her spirit. Turning on it with a holy indignation she cried: 'As the Lord lives, who is the beloved Spouse of my soul, you will be made to swallow down the thing for which you show such deep disgust.' So saying, she gathered into a bowl the water with which the ulcer had been washed and the corrupt matter which had come away with it, and going to one side she swallowed it."

The very next night, Christ rewarded Catherine's actions by appearing to her in a vision, with all five wounds from the crucifixion fully on display. According to Raymond, he said to Catherine:

"Yesterday the intensity of your ardent love for me overcame even the instinctive reflexes of your body itself: you forced yourself to swallow without a qualm a drink from which nature recoiled in disgust. In response to this I now say, that as you then went far beyond what mere human nature could ever have achieved, so I today shall give you a drink that transcends in perfection any that human nature can provide or has ever heard of." With that, Raymond says, Christ affectionately placed his right hand on her neck, and drew her mouth toward the wound in his side. "Drink, daughter, from my side," he said, "and by that draught your soul shall become enraptured with such delight that your very body, which for my sake you have denied, shall be inundated with its overflowing goodness." Catherine was enthusiastic, Raymond reported, fastening her lips on the wound and drinking from it as ravenously as if she were trying to quench some kind of mystic thirst.

Raymond described another vision that occurred a short time after Catherine supposedly first drank from Christ's side.

On a certain day, then, the Lord appeared to her as she was at prayer in her little cell, and told her of the coming of the new marvel into her life. "I am now making known to you beforehand, my daughter," he said to her, "the unwonted conditions under which the rest of your mortal life is to be lived out. The gifts I am now about to shower on you are so rare, that they will cause amazement and incredulity in the minds of ignorant and fleshly-minded men. Even your friends will come to doubt you, and suspect that you are the victim of delusions. But the root cause of all this will be the great love I bear you. For I intend to flood your soul with such an abundance of divine grace that its effects will brim over upon your very body, which will begin to take on an abnormal way of life, totally different from that of the common run of men. Besides this, your heart will now be so filled with burning zeal for the salvation of souls that you will lay aside the conventional restraints imposed upon women, and break entirely with the habits of reserve in this regard which you have trained yourself in up to this. Indeed, you are now to plunge boldly into public activity of every kind with but one thought in mind, the salvation of souls, whether they be men or women."

In one of her letters to Raymond, Catherine likened the open wound of Christ to an open treasure chest, full of fragrance: "Oh, flowing Source, which givest to drink and excitest every loving desire, and givest gladness, and enlightenest every mind and fillest every memory which fixes itself thereon! So that naught else can be held or meant or loved, save this sweet and good Jesus! Blood and fire, immeasurable Love!"

After the plague subsided, Raymond suggested they enjoy a respite in Montepulciano, a beautiful hilltop town about 40 miles southeast of Siena that held a special place in Raymond's heart, as he had served four years as a rector there. Raymond had told Catherine much about Agnes of Montepulciano, who had founded a Dominican convent. Born into a noble family in Italy in about 1268, Agnes early on convinced her reluctant parents to allow her to join a monastery at age nine. Her reputation for holiness soon spread, and she got by on nothing but bread and water for at least 15 years. She saw many visions of the Virgin Mary and Jesus before dying in 1317 at the age of 43, and miracles have been reported at her tomb. She was made a saint in 1726.

As legend has it, when Catherine went with Raymond to visit Agnes's tomb, she leaned over her incorrupt body. Suddenly the deceased saint raised her foot to meet Catherine's lips. Those in the room were astounded, but some were also quite angry at the idea that their very own Agnes would somehow pay deference to an outsider like Catherine.

Their time spent in Montepulciano dissipated any final doubts Raymond may have harbored about Catherine. Up until then, Raymond had not been wholeheartedly certain that all of Catherine's revelations were divine. But on that trip, Raymond received a mental vision of his own sins, one that left him so sad he broke down crying. Catherine spoke to him with such insight about God's forgiveness that he was convinced she must be Christ's true mouthpiece on earth.

Even so, the earnest Raymond was not always able to keep up with all that the energetic Catherine did and said, as he admitted with a measure of humor. On one occasion, when she was ventilating at great length, as she often did, on the divine mysteries of the world, he nodded off. "But she was all absorbed in God as she spoke, and went on with her discourse for a long time before she noticed that I was asleep," he wrote. "At last, she noticed it and then woke me up by saying with a loud voice, 'Ah, why do you lose your soul's profit by sleeping? Am I talking about God to a wall or to you?'"

The two of them would go through a great deal—but always together.

SIX

Bearing the Wounds of Christ

While in Siena sometime in mid-1374, 27-year-old Catherine received a surprise visit from a very important man: Alfonso da Vadaterra, a former bishop who had been spiritual director to Bridget of Sweden, perhaps the woman with a career path most comparable to Catherine's. Pope Gregory XI had sent the Spaniard from Avignon to get to know the young woman he had been hearing so much about. His assignment was to give Catherine the pope's blessing as well as ask her to use her influence to help ease tensions between the papacy and the Tuscan city-states. Bridget had served faithfully in the role of papal adviser and confidante, and her death in July 1373 had left a huge void that a grieving Gregory hoped to fill. Clearly, the pope had taken notice of Catherine's fame and scope of talents since her move into the public arena in 1368 and was curious to learn more about her abilities. As with Bridget, Gregory was looking for someone with a prophetic voice who might lend credence to papal policies. Catherine's name was probably first put forth as a possible replacement for Bridget by Raymond. He hadn't known her long, but he could already tell that Catherine's keen intelligence, engaging personality and way with words could serve as powerful tools of persuasion; if the pope was looking for a new Bridget, Raymond believed he had found her. Quite possibly, Catherine was first vetted for the role (whether she knew it or not) while attending the meeting of Dominicans in Florence in early 1374.

After her meeting with Vadaterra, a seemingly pleased Catherine wrote to Bartolomeo Dominici, one of her followers: "The pope sent his representative here, the one who was spiritual father to that countess who died in Rome. He is the one who for love of virtue renounced the episcopate, and he came to me in the holy father's name to say that I should offer special prayers for him and for the holy Church, in token of which he brought me the holy indulgence."

Vadaterra must have delivered a favorable report to Gregory, as the pope showed increased confidence in her from that time forward. Catherine's career and reputation were about to be shaped decisively by the political scene unfolding in Tuscany, particularly by the bubbling tensions between Florence and the papacy that ultimately led to the War of Eight Saints in 1375. That war, precipitated by the aggressiveness of the pope's legates in Italy, began with a Florence-led revolt against the papal states. With Gregory's backing, Catherine made one of her first major forays outside Siena—to Pisa in early 1375. It was an exhausting 80-mile journey that marked a radical enlargement of the very public role she had already taken on. It was practically unheard of for a woman to journey so far from her home. But not only had the Pisans asked her to visit, she also had been instructed to go to Pisa by representatives of Gregory, who hoped her presence there might shore up the town's loyalty to the papacy. Catherine was only too happy to make the trip, no matter how grueling it was, knowing full well that local governments would be less likely to support the idea of a crusade if they were entangled in battles with the pope or each other. A large group of male and female disciples, including Raymond, accompanied her on the trek, which took them many days by foot over roads that were little more than dusty, rough tracks. But the landscape was picturesque, and they would have traversed soft hills covered in olive groves and vineyards. It's quite possible that none of them traveled on horseback as Dominicans were not generally allowed to ride horses, unless in the company of royalty. In the public's mind horses were affiliated with nobility. Also making the trip was her mother, Lapa, who must have been in good health and who would have been desperate to stay close to her favorite child. Testifying to the great importance of the occasion, on hand to greet the group upon their arrival was the governor of Pisa, the archbishop and several other notable residents. While there, Catherine and the others were hosted in the comfortable homes of wealthy churchgoers. Everywhere she went she was scrutinized and stared at. She also received numerous requests by both letter and messenger, according to Raymond, from various groups in the city, all wanting her to minister to them. Ultimately she would spend nearly the entire year of 1375, off and on, in Pisa.

In the Middle Ages, the popular heroes were the saints, and this is how Catherine was greeted as she walked the streets of Pisa. She probably felt at home in this city of 50,000 that in many ways resembled her own hometown of Siena. Both cities, which had long operated in Florence's shadow, bore the imprint of Giovanni Pisano, the highly respected sculptor, painter and architect who had designed the façade of the duomo in Siena. Just a few years before, in 1372, the bell chamber had been completed on the leaning tower of Pisa that is so well known today. The tower was constructed as part of Pisa's column-filled Piazza dei Miracoli, one of the most astounding displays of Romanesque architecture in Italy. Watching as everyone fawned all over her, Raymond grew worried that the adoration might go to her head. Catherine reassured him that all the attention in the world meant nothing to her, and that she was interested only in currying favor with the Lord. Yet she must have somehow felt the prestige and the perks that come with carrying the pope's stamp of approval.

And soon she would also bear a much more fantastic distinction—the mark of Christ's suffering.

One day in Pisa, Catherine fell into a deep meditation, gazing upon the crucifix above the altar, just after receiving Holy Communion at the small Romanesque church of St. Christina. This was not out of the ordinary. Although she lay on the ground, face-down, stiff as a board, Raymond at first would have thought nothing of it. As always, he and the others stood by, chatting among themselves as they waited patiently for her to recover her senses. But after a long time passed, Raymond looked over and noticed that Catherine had risen up on her knees, still in a trance, with her arms outstretched and her eyes tightly shut. Then, just as suddenly, she slumped onto the floor.

He later described the episode: "Her face became radiant. For a long time she knelt like that, bolt upright, her eyes closed. Then, whilst we still looked on, all of a sudden she pitched forward on the ground as if she had received a mortal wound." After Raymond rushed to her side, Catherine recovered consciousness. She quietly turned to tell him what had just happened, "Father, I must tell you that, by his mercy, I now bear the stigmata of the Lord Jesus on my body." Raymond couldn't immediately see any signs of injury, but he instinctively knew that something incredible had just happened. Catherine told him: "I saw Our Savior on the cross lean down toward me in a bright light. And when my soul tried to hasten to meet its Creator, it forced my body to rise. Then I saw how five jets of blood came from the five wounds and streamed towards my miserable body. I cried out, 'O my Lord and Savior. I beg You, do not let the wounds on my body be visible outwardly'—and while I spoke the jets of blood changed to shining light, and as rays of light they struck my hands, feet and heart."

Although no one but Catherine could see the marks on her body, she told Raymond she had received the wounds of the crucified Christ, wounds so incredibly painful she wasn't sure how she'd be able to bear them without some sort of divine intervention. And indeed she spent a week in bed, barely able to move, which set a flurry of prayers into motion. Raymond and the others begged God to make her well, and he did. On Easter Sunday she felt energetic enough to get up and go to Mass at the Church of St. Christina. She told Raymond she derived strength from the wounds, even while acknowledging the ongoing pain.

Catherine never wrote about the stigmata incident in her letters, or even spoke publicly of it, but Raymond spread the story to followers and friends, who repeated it to countless others. The miraculous account left both believers and nonbelievers in its wake. Years later, after her death, the wounds were, according to some, finally visible. But only Catherine was able to see them during her lifetime. For her, receiving the stigmata was the culmination of a string of many mystical experiences that had begun when she was a child. Although the idea of spontaneously inflicted wounds of the crucified Christ suddenly showing up on one's skin leaves many scratching their heads, the stigmata became part of Catherine's legend, an occurrence that contributed greatly to her notoriety and reputation. Personally, the stigmata brought overwhelming comfort to Catherine, signifying her full participation in the death of Christ. "Remember Christ crucified,

God and man . . . Make your aim the Crucified Christ, hide in the wounds of the Crucified Christ and drown in the blood of the Crucified Christ," she wrote. Catherine had always been obsessed with Christ's blood and his suffering, and almost all of her letters opened with some reference to it.

Christ's Crucifixion was indeed horrific—and his suffering extreme—but the execution had actually gone better than his accusers had planned. Although Jesus disappointed those who wanted him to show superhuman power by coming down off the cross as the victorious King of Israel, he stayed put and died even faster than most crucifixion victims. Since no vital organs were damaged, death was usually painfully slow for anyone withering away on a cross. So horrendous was this form of punishment that the word "excruciating" derives from the Latin *excruciatus*—or "out of the cross." This barbarous penalty had been common among the Romans for at least 70 years, a perfectly designed castigation bound to strike fear in anyone even thinking about standing up against Rome or Roman laws. As with all condemned prisoners, Christ was raised to an upright position a few feet off the ground, and nails were pounded through his hands—or more likely between some bones in the wrist area—as well as his feet, in order to secure him to the cross. Slowly, he sagged down, putting more weight on the nails in his wrists, the pain shooting out along his fingers and up his arms to explode in his brain. The shoulders and elbows dislocated by popping out of joint, ripping ligaments. Soon the body reached the point of no return, and either his heart ruptured or he died from asphyxiation.

Described in all four Gospels, the story of the Crucifixion and the Resurrection is the underpinning miracle on which Christianity is built. Christians believe Jesus is the Son of God, sent to Earth to die for our sins. Therefore, the cross remains a powerful symbol of reconciliation with God through faith in Jesus, and Christians around the world commemorate the suffering every year on Good Friday through song, prayer, fasting, repentance and meditation. In the Middle Ages, people were less bothered by gruesome suffering, and, even today, the Crucifixion is believed to be the perfect atoning sacrifice for the sins of all people.

Through the centuries, many besides Catherine have claimed to bear on their bodies the stigmata. The term is ancient, appearing in the Apostle Paul's Epistle to the Galatians (6:17), in which he said, "I bear on my body the marks [stigmata] of Jesus." Biblical scholars still aren't sure, though, what marks Paul might have been referring to. The Greek word *stigma* means a mark, brand or tattoo. *Stigmata* is simply the plural. Numerous people—both Catholics and non-Catholics—say they have experienced the stigmata, and descriptions of the event have taken every form imaginable. Some people display only one or two markings, while others exhibit all the wounds that, according to the Gospels, were inflicted on Christ. These include not only the nail wounds to the hands and feet, but also the spear wound in the side as well as wounds on the head from the crown of thorns. Some cases of stigmata reportedly drag on for many years, while others occur and then are over in a matter of days. While some describe a continual bleeding from very obvious spots on the skin, others report feeling constant pain but without any evident marks. As Christian theologian Ivan Illich put it, "Compassion with Christ . . . is faith so strong and so deeply incarnate that it leads to the individual embodiment of the contemplated pain." Common among many stigmatics is the apparent ability to subsist with almost no water or food—beyond the Eucharist—for extended periods of time.

The first recorded case of stigmata occurred in 1224, when the wounds of Christ were spontaneously branded on the hands and feet of future saint Francis of Assisi two years before his death. Biographers say Francis had stopped to pray on Monte La Verna in Tuscany—which today is the site of a monastery—when he saw a vision of Christ crucified, in the form of a six-winged seraph, come down from the sky. While rapt in deep contemplation, Francis watched as the angel departed, leaving behind the signs of Christ's wounds on Francis's body.

Francis's fame ensured that news of his stigmatization would soon spread far and wide throughout Europe. Since 1224, many have referred to the event as a major miracle, while others have blasted it as a hoax. Today, evidence for the reality of stigmata has drawn an array of conclusions, with experts struggling to explain the phenomenon. Dr. Oscar D. Ratnoff, a well-known authority on blood clots, wrote that—after examining cases of stigmata—he still was not sure about the connection between emotional pressures and obviously organic results. He cited not only cases of stigmata in religious Christians, but also in Muslims bearing the wounds of the Prophet Muhammad in battle. Today's Catholic Church does not take an official position on the existence of stigmata, agreeing that miracles happen while not formally acknowledging even Francis's stigmata as a true miracle.

Beyond the stigmata, Catherine's lengthy stay in Pisa was notable for other reasons. Because she had healed many of the sick, more sick people soon arrived from surrounding areas. She was pushed and pulled in many directions and at one point was so exhausted she felt she couldn't get out of bed. Raymond and others sought the best remedy they knew (besides prayer) to help get her strength back: vernaccia, a white regional wine in a sea of red grapes known for its healing properties. When dabbed on a person's temples and wrists, the wine was supposed to bring almost instant relief. Catherine's friends tracked down a wine dealer who almost always stocked vernaccia and asked him to provide them with a decanter of it. "I would gladly give you the barrel if I had it," he replied, "but it has been empty for three months." For emphasis, he pulled the spigot from the barrel—and then stared in amazement as wine gushed out. Astonished but grateful, the group immediately brought some vernaccia to Catherine, who soon felt better. To her great embarrassment, news of the miracle spread fast and far so that when she was back on her feet, people greeted her with wonder—and skepticism. "Well, what do you know," someone teased. "You don't drink wine but you can fill an empty cask with it!" Disbelievers were always trying to trip her up, but she was typically able to win them over with her wit, faith and wisdom. Once, two scholars, a physician and a lawyer, asked to see her in Pisa, determined to catch her in some kind of falsehood. They posed a question: Since the Bible says God spoke aloud when creating the world, does that mean God has a mouth and a tongue? Her answer rendered them speechless: "I am amazed that you, who teach others, should come to seek instruction from a poor little woman like me, whose ignorance you should rather enlighten. It would be of very little purpose for me to know how God, who is Spirit and not a body, spoke in creating the world. What does matter both to me and to you is to know that Jesus Christ, the Eternal Word of God, took flesh and suffered to redeem us."

Not only was Catherine actively healing the sick while in Pisa, she also stubbornly continued to try to drum up support for the crusade against Islam. She dictated letters to Queen Mary of Hungary, Queen Giovanna of Naples and others. To Giovanna she wrote: "Oh what a great joy it will be to see you giving blood for blood! I would like to ask you to make this holy crusade— you in particular and all the other Christians who might want to join you. For if you stand up and declare your willingness to do this, and if you put your holy resolution into action, you will find Christians very willing to follow you. I beg you for love of Christ crucified to be zealous about this." Unlike male holy men during this time, who would have directed their words to other men, Catherine never underestimated the influence of women. Catherine wrote to Pope Gregory as well, begging him to do whatever it took to end any and all corruption within the church and especially to make peace with Florence and the other city-states so that the crusade could be his only focus.

Although the relationship between Florence and the pope had been troubled for years, at no time were those hostilities as overt as during the War of the Eight Saints, which lasted from 1375 to 1378. The conflict's name derived from the election of eight special priors granted broad authority to collect money to defend the city by paying off mercenaries—and much of that money was to come from local churches. Even though relations between Florence and the papacy had been uneven for decades, the conversation had been mostly cordial on both sides. Not anymore. Indeed, years of greed, arrogance and corruption displayed by the papal legates—not to mention Gregory's plans to gain control over as much land as possible in Tuscany—led Florentines to act out their frustrations by going on a tirade against papal aggression. They had plenty of ammunition. In the face of widespread food scarcity and famine—caused in large part by heavy flooding across Italy that had washed away much of the seed for new harvests—the pope's representative in Bologna, the ruthless Cardinal Guillaume de Noellet, tried to cripple Florence by refusing to grant permission for grain from areas under his charge to be shipped there. Even worse, he greedily tried to extort 60,000 florins from the Florentine Republic by threatening an attack by mercenaries if the leadership didn't comply. Outraged, the Florentines refused.

At times the pope tried to ease tensions, writing to the Florentines of his abiding affection for the people. Claiming he had only their best interests at heart, he urged them to negotiate an agreement with the cardinal so that they wouldn't be attacked. But soon the tables turned. The Florentines grew wise to the papacy's shenanigans and worked out their own deal with Sir John Hawkwood, who never liked de Noellet, agreeing to pay him 130,000 florins for assurances of a five years' peace with him. A few days later, the Florentines discovered what they believed to be a plot by a local monk working with the church to hand the town of Prato (then part of the province of Florence) over to Hawkwood. They captured the monk as well as another church official believed to be working with him and brutally tortured them to death in public. Whether or not there really was a plot isn't certain. But these episodes hardened Florence's stance toward the pope, making an all-out rupture in the relationship unavoidable. For his part, Hawkwood was satisfied with the deal he had brokered with the Florentines, and so happily set off to Pisa and Siena, where he managed to wrangle another 30,000 florins and 35,500 florins out of the cities, respectively, in exchange for his promise not to attack. Florence and its allies covered the costs by hiking taxes on the priests. From the pope's letters, it might have seemed as though he disapproved of de Noellet's actions, but a letter from Gregory to one of Hawkwood's marshals revealed that the pope himself was actually the mastermind behind the strategy. Gregory ordered him "to hinder the enemy from reaping the coming harvests, seeing that a deadly blow can now be inflicted; for if the enemy were to lose their harvests they would themselves be driven to act to the honour and profit of the pope."

As tensions continued to mount, the pope turned again to Catherine, who—after months in Pisa—was sent on another mission to

Lucca, a walled city of divided loyalties located just a short distance to the northeast, to persuade its leaders to support the pope. Everywhere she went, people raced outside to catch a glimpse of the Sienese woman so holy she could heal the sick and bring the near-dead back to life. Leaders in Lucca were anxious, caught in the middle of the pope's tug-of-war with Florence and not sure which way to be pulled. In this two-sided battle of words, Florence had put forth its eloquent and cultured chancellor, Coluccio Salutati, as its spokesman in Lucca. So confident was the pope in Catherine's capabilities that he allowed her, an uneducated and illiterate woman, to go head-to-head against Salutati's brilliant Latin rhetoric. It's not clear how often they met, but a series of dictated letters—the propaganda medium of the day—provides evidence that Catherine at least held her own against the learned chancellor.

Catherine's letters to the pope, too, were an elegant combination of forthrightness and sincerity. From Lucca, she warned Gregory that if he didn't better shoulder his myriad responsibilities, the terrible divides within the church would only become irrevocable breaks. Catherine also reported on her efforts to diminish tensions in a long letter to the pope.

She began as she usually did: "Your unworthy, poor and wretched daughter Caterina, servant and slave of the servants of Jesus Christ, is writing to you in his precious blood." She cautioned against the dangers of self-centeredness among church leaders: "Sometimes, it's just that they would like to keep the peace, and this, I tell you, is the worst cruelty one can inflict. If a sore is not cauterized or excised when necessary . . . not only will it not heal, but it will infect the whole body, often fatally." Referring to the pope as "my dear *babbo* [daddy]," she warned him not to be excessively soft. "A shepherd such as this is really a hireling! Not only does he fail to rescue his little sheep from the clutches of the wolf;

he devours them himself! And all because he loves himself apart from God. He does not follow the gentle Jesus, the true shepherd who gave his life for his little sheep."

Catherine concluded by urging, "If till now you haven't been very firm in truth, I want you, I beg you, for the little time that is left to be so—courageously and like a brave man—following Christ, whose vicar you are. And don't be afraid, father, no matter what may happen, of those blustery winds that have descended upon you—I mean those rotten members who have rebelled against you. Don't be afraid for divine help is near. Just attend to spiritual affairs, to appointing good pastors and administrators. Do something about it! . . . Pursue and finish with true holy zeal what you have begun by holy intent—I mean your return [to Rome] and the sweet holy crusade."

A short time after dictating this letter, she took Gregory to task again for his perceived failings to reach out and communicate more openly with the Italian city-states: "Forgive me, father, for talking to you like this. Out of the fullness of the heart the mouth speaks, you know . . . I beg you to communicate with Lucca and Pisa as a father, as God will teach you. Help them in any way you can and urge them to keep holding their ground. I have been in Pisa and Lucca until just now, and have pleaded with them as strongly as I could not to join the league with the rotten members who are rebelling against you. But they are very anxious, since they aren't getting any encouragement from you and are being constantly goaded and threatened by the other side."

All her pleas came to naught. In early 1376, the elders of Lucca opted to side with the anti-papal league, dealing a crushing blow to Catherine. She wrote of her disappointment to the governing magistrates, "I had been happy, jubilant, about the courage you'd had, up to now, to be strong and steadfastly obedient to holy

Church. But now, when I heard the opposite, I was really sorry . . . Don't get involved in such stupidity." But like domino pieces, the states of Italy began choosing war, with Lucca, Pisa and Siena all throwing in their lot with Florence. The Italian states were fed up, tired of the threats from mercenaries who had been sent to them by Avignon. The Florentine cause received another big boost in early 1376, when Bologna took the rebel cities' side. The Milanese ruler, Bernabo Visconti, also announced his alliance with Florence—a move that devastated Catherine, who had dictated a long letter to Visconti, imploring him to never "rebel against your head," meaning the pope. Catherine had even taken her case to Visconti's wife, Beatrice Regina della Scala, and asked for her help in influencing her husband. Referring to her as "dearest mother and sister in Christ," Catherine requested that she "challenge him, beg him with all of your might, to behave like a true servant and son of Christ crucified, to be obedient to the holy father, his representative, and to cease being rebellious." A response from Visconti or his wife does not exist, but it's obvious the ruler wasn't swayed by Catherine's passionate rhetoric. War, it finally seemed, was on the horizon, and Catherine's hopes for a crusade in the Holy Land would have to be shelved for the time being.

In the same letter in which she scolded Gregory for failing to communicate with the leaders of the Italian city-states, Catherine also had the gall to give the pope advice on the selection of cardinals. Her audacity must have floored Gregory. Almost no woman in the Middle Ages other than Catherine or Bridget of Sweden would have been so brazen as to give advice to a powerful man—let alone the pope. But the pope had riled Catherine by appointing nine new cardinals, three of whom were related to him in one way or another. In her letter Catherine didn't voice specific objections to any one appointment, but she did warn that when he made his decisions going forward, "I believe it would be in God's honor and better for you to be careful always to choose virtuous men. Otherwise it will be a great insult to God and disastrous to the holy Church." Dramatically, she ended her letter by emphasizing her great disappointment: "Oh, Father, I am dying of sorrow and cannot die."

Until then, Catherine's first priority, beyond saving souls, had been the crusade, but she now recognized that she was also needed as an instrument of papal policy. She offered her services to the pope's prelates, saying she could take the temperature of the people caught up in the hostilities between the papacy and the Tuscan city-states. She told one follower, "Don't be afraid . . . of the plots and attacks of the devils who might come to pillage and take over the city of your soul. No, don't be afraid, but be like knights drawn up on the battlefield, armed with the sword of divine charity." The bubbly daughter of a wool dyer had become a full-fledged militant, one who was laying the groundwork for future battles with a stirring call-to-arms—or moral summons.

And yet her devotion to the church and to the pope never turned a blind eye or deaf ear to their failings. She described the church as having an inflated sense of pride and a bloated ego. She likened selfish clergy to flies who taste the sweetness of Christ's blood but abandon their morality. "Not only does such inequity stink to me, but even the devils find this wretched sin repugnant," she said. And Catherine was just getting started.

This famous fresco by Andrea di Vanni, one of Catherine's disciples, is the oldest known picture of the saint.

This painting, Stigmatization of St. Catherine of Siena, by Domenico Beccafumi, depicts St. Catherine of Siena receiving the stigmata, or the signs of the cross.

This painting by Alessandro Franchi depicts a young Catherine defying her parents by cutting off her long hair.

Siena's San Domenico Church where Catherine worshipped. Credit: MM

The Fountain of Fontebranda, the oldest and most famous of the many fountains in Siena, located close to where Catherine grew up. Credit: MarkusMark

This painting by Giovanni di Paolo, St. Catherine Exchanging her Heart with Christ, *depicts Catherine exchanging her heart with Christ.*

The Ecstasy of St. Catherine of Siena *by Pompeo Batoni depicts Catherine in ecstasy.*

The painting The Mystic Marriage of St. Catherine of Siena *by Giovan Pietro Birago depicts the mystical marriage of Catherine.*

This painting by Giovanni di Paolo depicts Catherine holding white lilies.

Portrait of Pope Gregory XI, who was often counseled by Catherine of Siena.

Avignon, France, home to the pope from 1309 to 1378. Credit: Fr Antunes

Avignon's Palais des Papes, where the papacy was located from 1309 to 1378.

Panorama of Rome, Italy, where Catherine died in 1380. Credit: trialsanderrors

This painting by Girolamo di Benvenuto depicts the death of Catherine in 1380.

SEVEN

The Spilling of Blood

Catherine was obsessed with blood throughout her life. Not a day went by when she didn't dream of spilling her own, and there are at least 2,000 references to blood in her writings. In one letter, she expressed a desire to "sweat blood" to atone for all the sins of the world. In another, she called herself the "handiwork" of the Holy Trinity as a "new creation in the blood of your Son." The saint's thoughts about blood were as beguiling and intricate as the plasma and platelets running through her veins. She derived a bizarre pleasure from the physical substance, as if some primeval instinct was being satisfied. To Catherine, blood was synonymous with Christ, and it had the power to cleanse and forgive.

This all-consuming love of blood makes Catherine's intervention on behalf of a young Perugian prisoner named Niccolo di Toldo, who was the offspring of nobility—sentenced to death for a wine-infused evening of impetuous talk against Sienese leaders—all the more compelling.

It was June 1375, just a few months after Catherine had received the stigmata in April. In Pisa, the 28-year-old Catherine had been busy promoting the crusade against Muslims and seeking to persuade the Italian city-states not to break ties with the pope. She returned for a few weeks to Siena after she heard about a man who had been tried and found guilty of "sowing discord" in the city and of being "pernicious to the state of the present government." Perhaps he professed attachment to the wrong person or somehow fanned the flames of discontent; no one knows the specifics of his crime. His punishment, however, "according to the full rigor of the law," was clear: beheading. Both decapitation and hanging were common forms of capital punishment in medieval Europe. The aims of these barbarous public displays were twofold: first, to shock spectators and, as a result, suppress dissent, and second, to reaffirm the government's authority. So long as the axe was sharp, beheadings were so clean and swift that they were actually considered a privileged way to die and reserved mainly for members of the nobility.

At the time, Siena was sympathetic with those republics in collusion against the papacy. However, the city of Perugia, north of Rome, was pro-pope, and it seemed that Niccolo might have been in Siena trying to help those parties favorably inclined toward the papacy. Perhaps Niccolo was working with Gérard du Puy, the greatly detested papal governor and relative of the pope who was considered the single greatest enemy of the Sienese regime. This regime—the Riformatori—was doing all it could to put down unrest during this period, which helps explain Niccolo's arrest and conviction for what might otherwise have been a somewhat minor offense. At first the church protested Niccolo's harsh sentence, but eventually it stood back and asked only that he be treated mercifully. Catherine also tried to persuade the authorities to reverse their decision, but even she had no luck.

In what is no doubt one of her most powerful and emotional letters, Catherine relayed to Raymond the entire story of how she visited and converted Niccolo and even accompanied him to his execution. Her recollection, sprinkled with professions of affection for the apparently handsome young man, reads almost like some wild romance and culminates in a metaphorical marriage on the scaffold.

It's not clear how Catherine, who was in Pisa, first heard about Niccolo, but we do know that both she and Raymond were somehow familiar with the man because she referred to Niccolo in her letter to Raymond as "the one you know" facing execution. She must have traveled full tilt from Pisa to Siena, as executions were typically carried out very soon after authorities imposed the punishment. Once in Siena, she met up with Tommaso Caffarini, her Dominican follower and second hagiographer, and the two went together to visit Niccolo in his cell. Previously, he had turned away any priest or anyone else interested in trying to save his soul. They found him in a frenzy, completely beside himself. So enraged was he over being wrongly accused that he wanted nothing whatsoever to do with God. As Caffarini put it, he was pacing his cell "like a ferocious and desperate lion." But then Catherine arrived, and, within minutes, his demeanor softened. As Niccolo basked in the warmth of her presence, he was soothed by a confidence in her voice, one that seemed at odds with the frailness of her body.

Catherine told him that faith in God was the only direct route to a freedom far sweeter than anything he could ever know on earth, and that God would forgive all his sins if only he sincerely asked for his mercy. She reminded him that Christ too was an innocent man, crucified on a cross for all to see. Niccolo hung on to her every word and then cried.

Before Catherine left, Niccolo made her promise that, "for the love of God," she would return the next morning and be with him at the time of his execution. He could bear what was to come, he claimed, only if she was at his side. Very early the next morning, before the bell signaling the end of the overnight curfew rang out from the tower in Siena, Catherine hastily made her way to Niccolo's cell. At the sight of her, he smiled, relieved that she'd come following his long solitary night. The two attended Mass together and he received the Eucharist, something he had not done once in the many years since his first Communion. He confessed his fear that any and all vows of bravery might evaporate in the moments before death. But when Catherine assured him again that she would be with him at the place of execution, right by his side, these apprehensions melted away. "His head was resting on my breast," she wrote. "I sensed an intense joy, a fragrance of his blood—and it wasn't separate from the fragrance of my own, which I am waiting to shed for my gentle spouse Jesus."

Catherine told Raymond that Niccolo conquered his fear of death with the help of God's goodness: "God's measureless and burning goodness tricked him, creating in him such an affection and love in the desire of God that he did not know how to abide without God."

The erotic tension of this interchange was palpable, and, even to the two of them, a certain intimacy must have been evident. She served both as lover and mother, calming him with her words and caressing his head as it rested against her breast. She listened to him. She prayed with him. And she made sense of what was happening by thinking of it all as a ploy by God, who she believed was using the man's affection for her to help him gain another lamb—another soul—in heaven.

Gently holding Niccolo, she whispered, "Courage, my dear brother, for soon we shall reach the wedding feast. You will go to it bathed in the sweet blood of God's son, with the sweet name of Jesus, which I don't want ever to leave your memory." With consummation fast approaching, she told him, "I shall be waiting for you at the place of execution."

Bright with joy, he looked at her and asked, "What is the source of such a grace for me, that my soul's sweetness will wait for me at the holy place of execution?" The realization that Niccolo had evolved to the point that he could consider the place of his execution as "holy" filled Catherine with pride.

Niccolo promised that he would go joyful and strong, "and when I think that you will be waiting for me there, it will seem like a thousand years until I get there!"

He followed this with "such tender words as to make one burst at God's goodness!" Catherine wrote.

And so the besotted pair parted—he in a cart and she on foot to the place of execution. Usually the prisoner's "comforter" would ride in the cart with him, but for some reason that didn't happen. Maybe it was deemed inappropriate for women—even for Catherine. Whether one sees Catherine's role as that of a priest, friend or imaginary lover, her presence during Niccolo's decapitation was, in fact, an example of a "comforting" ritual—or the practice of ministering to prisoners about to be executed—that became institutionalized in the fourteenth century. Unlike today, prisons in the Middle Ages did not have chaplains. Since the eternal salvation of the prisoner was paramount, it was the comforter's duty to prepare him to make his final confession and to receive the Eucharist. In this case, Tommaso Caffarini heard Niccolo's confession and presented him with the Eucharist while Catherine prayed with him and comforted him.

Catherine arrived first and climbed up onto the platform. She had long pined for martyrdom for herself, but it was Niccolo, a man she had just met, who was going to achieve it, or something very close to it. As she looked down upon the block where Niccolo would soon place his neck, she couldn't help but feel pangs of jealousy as she imagined her own neck there.

She took no notice of the people gathering around the execution site as she moved closer to it. She later said that—at this moment—she sensed only the presence of Catherine of Alexandria, a beheaded martyr she had long revered. Catherine gingerly knelt down, placing her own head on the block. As she described it: "I knelt down and stretched my neck out on the block, but I did not succeed in getting what I longed for up there."

At last the cart carrying Niccolo arrived. He descended "like a meek lamb" and, seeing Catherine waiting for him, laughed, as if she were the most incredible sight he had ever seen. He asked her to make the sign of the cross over him, and—of course—she did.

They fixed their gaze upon one another. She took his hand and led him to the block, telling him, "Down for the wedding, my dear brother, for soon you will be in everlasting life!" He did as he was told, albeit "very meekly." She described the events that followed: "I placed his neck [on the block] and bent down and reminded him of the blood of the Lamb. His mouth said nothing but 'Jesus' and 'Catherine' and as he said this, I received his head into my hands, saying 'I will' [or 'I want it'] with my eyes fixed on divine Goodness." The words were spoken almost as a marital vow and, after the axe came down, she caught his severed head in her arms.

She had completed her duties. Spattered with blood, she felt perfectly fulfilled but still a bit envious. As she wrote, "Now that he was hidden away where he belonged, my soul rested in peace and quiet in such a fragrance of blood that I couldn't bear to wash away his blood that had splashed on me . . . Poor wretch that I am, I don't want to say any more! With the greatest envy I remained on earth."

After seeing a vision of Niccolo's soul rising up to heaven, Catherine was able to rest easy. She watched as Jesus received it and placed it in the "open shop of his side," bringing the beheaded prisoner into total union with the crucified Christ. Somehow, by being joined into a union with Jesus, Niccolo's gender was transformed. As Catherine wrote, "He made a sweet gesture which would charm a thousand hearts . . . He turned as does a bride when, having reached her husband's threshold, she turns her head and looks back, nods to those who have attended her, and so expresses her thanks."

When relaying what she believed to be the meaning behind her vision to Raymond, Catherine remarked that "the first stone is already laid," an image that she might have conjured up in connection with the martyrs. In her mind, the martyrs were the stones on which the church is built. According to hagiographer Arrigo Levasti, the idea of the crusade was still planted firmly in her mind. Therefore, he said, Catherine looked at Niccolo's "blood spilled like red gems upon her white habit" as a harbinger of the blood that would soon be shed by Christians fighting against the infidels.

Catherine concluded her letter with an exhortation for Raymond to be filled with as much passion as Niccolo: "So do not be surprised if I impose on you only my desire to see you drowned in the blood and fire which pours out of the side of Christ." In other words, Niccolo's death should be seen as a model for Raymond to follow, an example of how to achieve a life in complete union with Christ through total commitment to him.

To Raymond, Catherine audaciously scripted herself as both the bride at the wedding—or execution—and Christ's proxy in Niccolo's conversion. To do as Catherine wished, Raymond would have to transform his gender to become—like Niccolo—the wife of the bridegroom Christ. By placing female flesh in such a prominent position, Catherine was once again asserting her authority.

Catherine's letter about Niccolo was among the first—if not the first—she ever wrote to Raymond. Since their first meeting in Florence the year before, she and Raymond had seldom been apart. But it appears that Raymond may not have accompanied her to Siena. Unlike her messages to other correspondents, Catherine's letters to Raymond frequently included long and very descriptive narrative passages outlining her life's most pivotal experiences. In one way, Catherine, through a masterful maneuvering of epistolary custom, actively helped write her own hagiography by recounting her saintly deeds in every glorious detail to her older and more educated future biographer. Oddly enough, Raymond never mentioned the story of Niccolo in his biography of Catherine, which was designed to advance the case for her canonization. Perhaps this formal son of Neopolitan nobility had been taken aback by the bold and somewhat crude language she used. Or maybe he thought such an emotional and passionate letter from a young woman about a young man would muddy her chances of achieving sainthood.

As the American theologian Benedict M. Ashley once wrote, Catherine derived her wonderful courage—which is perhaps her most prized personal characteristic—from her feeling that the very blood of Christ was coursing through her own veins. The brave Catherine's dramatic moment with Niccolo proved to her followers that she wasn't afraid of death. Catherine had been fearless, and it was with similar fearlessness that she approached her next challenges.

No matter what, Catherine never forgot about the push for a new crusade. But for her, as for the pope, this objective had become intrinsically linked to two other goals: the return of the papacy to Rome and the reunification of Italy, which remained torn apart by conflict between many of the city-states and the pope. Almost all of Catherine's energies throughout her lifetime would be channeled into these three concerns in one way or another.

From her base in Pisa, where she had spent the bulk of 1375, she had tried to drum up support in Italy for the crusade. She continued firing off one letter after another, seeking to secure backing from both average citizens and those in power. One such plea to Mariano d'Oristano, who ruled the island of Sardinia, garnered an auspicious pledge to join the crusade in person and to supply two galleys, 1,000 horsemen and 3,000 foot soldiers for a period of ten years. But he would never be required to make good on that promise.

Month after month, the political horizon in Italy grew darker and darker. The lowering clouds included the matter of the cardinals who were appointed in 1375, most of whom were French. Only one was Italian. Gregory's pick of cardinals seemed to be made in direct opposition to Catherine's intentions of persuading the pope to leave Avignon. Certainly the move did nothing to endear the pope to the Italians, who felt almost no affinity for the French and so certainly didn't want to see an increasing number of them as legates and governors of ecclesiastical provinces in Italy.

People everywhere were losing confidence in Gregory's leadership. There was a time when Gregory's rise in the ranks of the church might have been considered brilliant. The nephew of Pope Clement VI, Gregory was just 40 when he was elected pontiff. But despite being extremely well educated, he proved to be irresolute, and it became clear that his election was solely the result of nepotism. Although Gregory wasn't overtly opposed to going back to Rome at some point, the cardinals and members of his court had grown used to their comfortable lifestyle in France and therefore resisted the idea of returning to a place where discipline was more strictly enforced. Among their many appeals against going to Rome, one of the most persuasive, apparently, was the cardinals' complaint: "But Burgundy will not be there!" Everyone knew that Italian wines were inferior to French ones. And living inside the mighty walls of the Palace of the Popes—the lavishly decorated fortified palace that housed the papacy in Avignon—was a real treat. The Great Chapel and Library housed an impressive 2,000 books, which attracted a steady stream of artists, scholars and musicians from all over Europe. With 15,000 square meters of living space, the palace was equivalent to four Gothic cathedrals. Throughout the entire compound, excess and spiritual compromise reigned supreme. No doubt it was a hard place for members of the pope's court to leave. And even Gregory, who at least entertained the notion of returning to Italy, feared the volatility of the Romans and their reaction to a French pope and his French curia. As a result, he equivocated. In March 1376 an exasperated Catherine wrote again to Gregory: "My dear father! I am begging you. I am telling you: come! . . . In the name of Christ crucified I am telling you! Don't choose to listen to the devil's advisors. They would like to block your holy and good resolution. Be a courageous man for me, not a coward. Respond to God, who is calling you to come and take possession of the place of the glorious shepherd, Saint Peter, whose vicar you are."

By early 1376, Pisa and Lucca had lined up alongside anti-papal Florentine forces. The Florentines even tried to get the Romans to turn their backs on the pope, but they refused. Gregory sought to pull everyone back from the brink of disaster by dispatching ambassadors to Florence. But he was his own worst enemy. Accompanying the ambassadors was a forceful papal bull, or edict, demanding that the Florentines immediately surrender all members of their rebellious government into his hands.

Catherine again went into action, writing to the pope, repeating earlier warnings that he should not do anything to give his people an excuse for going to war with him: "My soul, which is united with God, burns with thirst for your salvation, for the reformation of the church, and the happiness of the whole world. But it seems to me that God reveals no other remedy than peace." She also defended the cause of the rebellious Florentines, saying, "I beg you from Christ crucified, and I demand that you do me this favor, overcome your wickedness by your goodness." Increasingly, Catherine's letters expressed her absolute certainty that she was the mouthpiece of the crucified Lord and that there was no reason for her not to write "I demand" and "You are to do as I advise you." Return to Rome, she said to the pope, and launch the crusade, and you will see the fearsome wolves transform themselves into weak little lambs. "Peace, peace, peace . . . and if you consider that justice demands revenge, strike me and let me suffer all the tortures and agonies you wish—even death. I believe it is the infection of my sins which is largely the cause of this misery and anarchy, so punish your little daughter as much as you will. Oh, Father, I am dying of sorrow and cannot die," she wrote.

In a letter to the much-feared Gérard du Puy, Catherine didn't mince words either: "Our Lord holds in aversion three detestable vices above all others—they are impurity, avarice and pride. And they all reign in the spouse of Christ—at least among her prelates, who seek after nothing but pleasures, honors and riches. They see the demons of hell carrying off the souls confided to them, and they care nothing at all about it." She then went on to tell him what to do about it: "And when the time comes for choosing pastors and cardinals, let not flattery and money and simony have any part in their election; regard nothing but the good qualities of the persons proposed, and give no heed whether they are nobles or peasants. Virtue is the only thing which really makes a man noble, or pleasing to God."

Catherine also had a thing or two to say to the Florentines. She urged them to seek forgiveness and to reconcile with the pope no matter what the cost. In a letter to Niccolo Soderini, the wealthy Florentine merchant she had become acquainted with during her time there, she wrote: "You know that a member cut off from its head cannot live, for it is not joined with the source of its life. It is the same, I tell you, with people cut off from God's love and charity. You know what I'm talking about. Now who are we—poor, miserable, proud, and wicked as we are—that we should act against our head."

But the Florentines—still seething over the pope's denial of their request for grain during the crop shortage of 1374 and a litany of other grievances—were not going to be swayed, not even by Catherine. At least on the surface, they were dead set on war, and they finally had the leaders of Pisa, Lucca and even Bologna in their corner.

Eventually, a fed-up Gregory issued an ultimatum to the leaders of Florence: either they appear before him in Avignon in person or they face dire consequences. Implied was the threat of interdict, which would mean the shuttering of all churches and the excommunication of all government members in Florence. While Florentines were far from ready to forgive and forget, that kind of warning brought cooler heads to the fore. City leaders decided to at least go through the motions of conciliation so they couldn't be blamed later for intransigence. At the very least, they would hear Gregory out—but they needed someone with an exemplary reputation who had the pope's ear to serve as an intermediary. Catherine of Siena was, of course, the perfect candidate. She was well regarded, close by and had the ear not only of the pope but also of powerful people in Florence. However, because she was a woman, and a young woman at that, leaders in Florence felt Raymond, her seasoned confessor who had successfully held several positions of responsibility, might be a better option. And so they asked him to go on Catherine's behalf. Raymond quickly set off, spending time in Florence and then in Pisa before heading on to Avignon.

While Raymond was gone, Catherine saw several potent visions that, she later said, helped her make sense of the rebellion against the pope and to understand why this type of discord was allowed to unfold under God's watchful eye. The answer, she said, was simple: it was love. God allowed evil to happen so that love could rise up and conquer it.

Despite Florence becoming more conciliatory, Gregory made good on his threat by announcing on the last day of March 1376 that Florence and its allies would indeed be placed under interdict. Catherine and others feared that the move was a recipe for war. Attending public worship and receiving sacraments were both explicitly prohibited. Any debts and loans owed to Florence were canceled; an embargo was slapped on Florentine goods. Citizens of Florence who traveled outside their city's borders could be captured or imprisoned—and there was nothing the church could do about it. For a mercantile city like Florence, these new rules were the equivalent of a death sentence. Catherine tried to mediate with the help of those Florentines worried that economic sanctions could stretch into months or years—and who now wanted to explore ways to reconcile. She traveled to Florence again, accompanied by her secretary Stefano Maconi. The city's leaders gave her a warm welcome when she arrived and seemed to grasp the importance of all that she had to say. But nothing she did could stop the papal interdict from being formally enforced. Churches were closed and locked inside a now hunkered-down city trying to ride out the economic sanctions. Catherine was disheartened, to say the least. While some Florentines remained openly defiant, others were inclined—in the face of the interdict—to at least consider hearing the pope out. An official delegation was readied to go to Avignon to see what terms might be worked out with the pope in exchange for peace. Catherine made her own hasty preparations, determined to get to Avignon first. She left Florence the last week of May 1376, accompanied again by Maconi and some Mantellate women. The journey, on foot and then by boat across the Ligurian Sea, took about three weeks. Travel was painfully slow in the Middle Ages. Even so, a small group with decent horses could travel as much as 30 miles in a single day.

It made little difference that Raymond was there already; Catherine had long wanted to go to Avignon and took it upon herself to make it happen. There were many things she wanted to discuss—in person—with the pope. Not only was there the matter of the defiant Florentines, but also the prospect of the crusade, church reform and the pope's possible return to Rome.

Traveling along the winding Rhône River, Catherine and her group—which included several priests—would have passed high cliffs of white limestone, fragrant fruit orchards and Roman ruins before coming around a final bend to the fabled St. Bénézet Bridge in Avignon. That bridge, built in 1282, spanned nearly 3,000 feet and was the only feasible crossing of the Rhône between the Mediterranean Sea and the French city of Lyon. Previously, people had made their way across the river in small boats, a precarious excursion that cost many lives over the years. It was said that Catherine had a preternatural ability to smell sin. In the presence of her male followers, she could tell which of them had succumbed to carnal desires with just one inhalation. She would scold the guilty party and promptly send them off to confession. Now, as she stepped off the boat at Avignon on June 18, 1376, one can presume she sampled the air and then quickly turned up her nose. She would have wanted to speak to the pope and then get away from there as soon as humanly possible.

Every opulent trapping of papal power was on display in Avignon. The palace, built between 1335 and 1364, occupied an area of 2.6 acres. The building was enormously expensive and had consumed much of the papacy's income during its construction. The palace rises behind the medieval ramparts, built in 1355, that surround the city.

The book *Avignon in Flower* by Marzieh Gail gives us some idea of what Avignon was like back then with her description of the pope setting off from the palace on a cavalcade to a neighboring estate:

There were the pope's white palfreys [riding horses highly val-ued in the Middle Ages], led by a groom, equerries carrying the pallium, or white wool band worn by the Pontiff as a symbol of might—and three red hats set on poles. Then would come two papal barbers, each holding a red case, one containing the pope's garments, the other his tiara in its box. After a sub deacon hold-ing up the cross, followed by a horse or mule bearing the Corpus Christi . . . then came the pope himself on a white horse, half a dozen nobles around him holding a canopy over his head, behind him an equerry carrying a montatorium to help him mount or dismount. A great crowd of courtiers, prelates and members of

the pope's household were next, the most useful being, perhaps,
the pope's almsgiver whose function was to break up traffic jams
by scattering little coins.

It is unlikely that Catherine would have even remotely enjoyed
the pomp and circumstance of the spectacle or that she would
have been impressed by the city's finery. Although she revered the
papacy and looked forward to meeting the pope, Avignon symbolized for her the dissipation and corruption that were chipping
away at the very soul of the church. The city was the epitome of
human excess.

For its part, those in Avignon were both suspicious of and in-
trigued by their famous female visitor. People had been gossiping
about Catherine—both on the streets and in palace hallways—
for weeks. The pope had arranged for her and her entourage to
stay in an elegant mansion that had once belonged to a cardinal:
"a fine house with a beautifully decorated chapel," according to
Stefano Maconi. Raymond, who had been in Avignon for some
time as part of an advance party, showed them around town.

Two days after her arrival, Catherine was graciously received
by the pope. "I desire nothing but peace," he told her. "I place the
affair entirely in your hands . . . only I recommend to you the honor
of the Church." Raymond, acting as an interpreter since Catherine
didn't speak French and Gregory didn't speak Italian, wrote that
what Catherine was about to say left Gregory speechless.

EIGHT

The Move to Rome

Convinced that Catherine was God's true agent on earth, the pope behaved as putty in her hands on that visit in 1376. She spoke sternly to Gregory as a parent might to an insubordinate child, denouncing the abuses practiced by priests and legates in the field that she claimed were corroding the very soul of the institution. She didn't hold her tongue either when talking about the papal court, railing against the corruption and immorality that were burgeoning under Gregory's own nose. At one point, the flustered pontiff interrupted her: "How have you, who have been here such a short time, got such knowledge of all that goes on here?"

Catherine looked straight into his eyes and said, "To the glory of Almighty God I am bound to say that I smelled the stink of the sins which flourish in the papal court while I was still at home in my own town more sharply than those who have practiced them, and do practice them, every day here."

As noted, Catherine was said to have had the gift—as did some other saints—of seeing and even smelling the beauty or the ugliness of a soul, meaning she was able to discern the state of a person's spirit as soon as she was in their company. Once, back in Siena, a revered lady, one seemingly full of virtue who was highly respected, dropped by for a visit. Catherine wouldn't so much as look at her, turning her back any time she came near. Raymond admonished her for her rudeness, but Catherine replied: "If you had smelled the stink of her sins you would have done the same." Some time later Raymond learned that Catherine was right: this woman was living as a priest's mistress.

Gregory was so impressed by the deep spiritual insight of Catherine, who had sent him at least six very candid letters before they had even met, that he granted her free rein to handle any and all papal negotiations with the Florentines. She was honored. But the ambassadors from Florence, who were supposed to follow on her heels, never showed up. On July 26 she wrote to those who had previously expressed regret for having gone against the church, asking them to prove their sincerity. By this time, she had gotten wind of a new tax placed by the Florentines on the clergy, leading her to believe the Florentines had changed their minds about wanting peace. "I have spoken with the Holy Father, and he has listened to me with great mildness . . . He has shown that he truly loves peace and that as a good father he is willing to overlook the offences which his sons have committed against him, but it is necessary for the sons to humiliate themselves so that the father can forgive them completely. I cannot tell you how happy I was when after a long conversation with me he said that he was willing to receive his children and to do what I thought best," she wrote. She urged the ambassadors to get there as soon as possible. An angry Gregory suggested that perhaps the Florentines were playing them for fools—suspicions that proved to be right. On July 6, a new government had been set up in Florence with leaders who were not in nearly as much of a hurry to make amends as the old ones had been. Later, they did dispatch three ambassadors to Avignon, but only as part of a ruse to cover up the new government's true designs.

Waiting for the Florentines, Catherine was received several times by the pope, which afforded her plenty of opportunity to talk to him about the issues she held most dear. Fortunately for her, Gregory had never been averse to the idea of eventually return-ing to Rome while also expanding the papal properties through-out Italy. But the idea had unnerved at least some in Florence who were not keen on the possibility of having their property taken over by the church. With Catherine on the scene, the political winds seemed to be shifting faster than expected, making the Avi-gnon contingent increasingly uneasy.

One day, according to Raymond, the irresolute Gregory asked Catherine to remind him again why he should return to Rome—perhaps just as an extra dose of reassurance. This time, she played the part of a coy young lady, noting that it would be unseemly for her to give advice to the Vicar of Christ. Irritated, he shot back that he only desired to know the will of God, not her opinion on the matter. Catherine replied: "Who knows God's will so well as your Holiness, for have you not bound yourself by a vow . . . fulfill what you have promised to God." Slightly shaken, Gregory just stared at her. As a cardinal, he had made a solemn vow to return the papacy to Rome if he were ever elected pope—but it was made in private. According to various hagiographical compilations, he had never told a living soul about it. From that moment on, Greg-ory, the seventh Avignon pope, knew he was destined to leave the country he knew so well. He also knew there would be enormous obstacles, even dangers, to overcome along the way.

Proof of this was an anonymous letter he had received—apparently the handiwork of French cardinals hoping to keep him in Avignon—warning that he would be poisoned if he ever went back to Rome. When he showed it to Catherine, she remained unfazed. "I conclude that the letter sent to you does not issue from the servant of God who has been named to your Holiness, nor that it was written from far away, but that it comes from near at hand, from the servants of the devil who have little fear of God," she said.

Again, the pope was amazed by the backbone of this delicate woman, even if others weren't so sure.

Even after having proved herself capable of great things, again and again, there were still some who tried to catch Catherine in their snare—but they might as well have been trying to throw a horse. The list of cynics was topped by the ambitious Duke of Anjou, brother of King Charles V, who was dead set on keeping the pope in France so that the country might retain its moral edge over its enemy, England. Visiting the pope, the duke couldn't believe how much sway this uneducated young woman held over him. He spoke for countless others in France when he vigorously resisted the idea of Gregory's "abandoning" Avignon. "You are traveling to a people and to a country where there is little love for you," the duke said. "You may indeed cause great harm to the church, for, were you to die there, which your doctors say is quite likely, the Romans—those alien and treacherous people— will control the Sacred College and will elect a pope who suits them." He pandered to Gregory's fearful nature by emphasizing the duplicity of the Italian people, a clever but ultimately unsuccessful tactic. When that didn't work, the duke decided it was Catherine he needed to win over. He invited her to his castle for a few days on the pretense of needing her to comfort his sickly wife. But rather than changing her mind, it was the duke who found himself won over by her argument for a crusade. Seeming to have forgotten the whole issue of the pope's location, he promised that if a crusade ever did happen, he would wholeheartedly commit himself to this holy cause.

Many weeks behind schedule, the three Florentine ambassadors finally turned up in Avignon, impolite and insolent. When Catherine told them that the pope had empowered her to represent him in peace negotiations, they balked. They had come to Avignon to speak with the pope and not some unlettered understudy. Catherine persisted even when the pope relented and appointed two French cardinals to try to negotiate with them. But, as Gregory suspected, the ambassadors weren't really interested in mutually agreed-upon solutions, even as the interdict wreaked economic havoc on their region. The talks quickly broke down, and in September the Florentine ambassadors were asked to leave. Once home, they gave their version of what had transpired, which persuaded Florence's leaders to stay the course with an eye toward suppressing the church's temporal power. If anything, the meeting caused them to harden their tone even more while enlisting even greater anti-papal support throughout Italy.

From Catherine's point of view, if Gregory returned the papacy to Rome, the Florentines would be forced to accept his authority and would soon fall in line. Even Gregory, who was known for his vacillating nature, grew more and more convinced that a return to Rome was inevitable.

And so, finally, in early September 1376, Gregory formally announced that he would leave Avignon. At least 22 ships were prepared and equipped in Marseille, a port city in southern France, ready to set sail at a moment's notice. Items belonging to the pope and some two dozen cardinals, as well as their staff members, were packed up. Goodbyes were said. Aides were dispatched to Italy to let the Romans know the pope was headed their way. Everything was in place. The day of departure finally came on September 13. Gregory left the papal palace for the last time as a mournful crowd stood by, looking on as if they were attending his funeral. As the pope reached the door, he came upon his elderly father, Count Guillaume de Beaufort, sprawled on the ground in protest. The father declared that "before my son departs . . . he shall pass over my body." The pope didn't flinch. He stepped over his father without hesitation and made his way onto the waiting ships. At least six cardinals opted to stay behind—refusing to leave their castles and connections—but most joined the papal entourage in spite of their misgivings about the dangers awaiting them in Rome. The papal cavalcade took off, traveling overland to Marseille before setting sail for Italy on October 2.

The seas were uncharacteristically rough—a bad omen for a group that was looking for any excuse to turn back. The cardinals were convinced that the storms were God's way of telling them they should return to Avignon. But the pope kept his nerve and, after moving slowly from port to port along the narrow coastal strip known as the Riviera, he and his party finally reached the regal city of Genoa on October 18. Having hurried off earlier, Catherine and her companions were already there. After settling in, the pope didn't waste any time confirming her whereabouts. Once he did, Gregory disguised himself in a simple black cassock and stealthily made his way across town to where she was staying that night. It was late and pitch black when he knocked on her door. She was surprised but thrilled to see him and knelt reverently at his feet in the doorway. The two of them then went off into a room together with only Raymond to translate, shutting the door behind them.

Raymond exercised absolute discretion. The nighttime rendezvous does not appear in his hagiography, yet the account has shown up in the works of Rawley Myers and other Catholic historians. Out of desperation, the sovereign pontiff had crept out alone, late at night, to seek the guidance of his unschooled adviser. Gregory had good reason to be panicky. He had heard rumors of riots in Rome as well as of the increasing violence in the war with Florence. One rumor that proved true had the Florentines decimating a band of soldiers sent by pro-pope Queen Giovanna of Naples. It was enough to make Gregory wonder whether he'd done the right thing. That's why he needed to see Catherine. Only her absolute conviction would be enough to fortify his courage. And she was indeed convinced. She encouraged him, comforted him and prayed with him—as no one else could—until he once more regained his emotional footing. The assuaged pontiff put his hooded mantle back on and skulked back into the darkness of the night. They never saw each other again.

The boats were readied and the papal party departed again on October 28, this time headed for Rome. Catherine set off about a week later, but not before she dictated a letter to Lapa back in Siena, who was apparently "falling to pieces" with worry over her daughter's safety. Catherine tried to console her while also exhorting Lapa—yet again—to reach deep inside herself to find the same kind of strength and courage Mary showed when letting go of her son, Jesus.

"You know that I must follow God's will, and I know that you want me to follow it. It was God's will that I go away . . . and my going was not without mystery, nor without worthwhile results. And so I must go in the future, following in his footsteps however and wherever it shall please his boundless goodness," she wrote. Catherine respected her mother enough to appreciate and accept her insecurities, but their relationship had shifted. Catherine was no longer the dutiful daughter but someone whose opinion carried weight with the pope. She wouldn't allow even her mother to get in her way. Her obedience was to God and no one else.

In November 1376, Catherine and her band of followers continued their journey by ship, sailing from Genoa to Livorno before walking the last 16 miles or so to Pisa over the course of a few days. Catherine's secretary, Stefano Maconi, went on ahead to Siena, where he delivered messages from Catherine to worried friends and family. Lapa, meanwhile, hurried in the other direction to be reunited with her daughter. Catherine, Lapa and the followers set up house inside a living space at the hospital next to the Church of St. Cristina in Pisa, happy to again be on Italian soil.

Meanwhile, Gregory was preparing himself for his return to Rome. His ships arrived just north of the city in mid-November. After two months of arduous negotiations, the Romans agreed to the pope's return, even going so far as to assure him that he'd be granted all the same rights and powers enjoyed by previous popes. After celebrating Christmas at Corneto, the pope landed at Ostia on January 13, 1377. He then sailed up the Tiber, the second-longest Italian river after the Po, to Rome. With trumpets blaring, the pope marched into the city on January 17, 1377, accompanied by nearly 2,000 armed men. After receiving the keys to the city, the pope headed up a festive procession that included dancers, musicians, knights and soldiers, barons, bishops and clergy, all dressed in their finest garb. Catherine hated all the pomp and circumstance and had wanted him to enter the city humbly, carrying only a cross. Almost all the states of Italy—even those still at war with the papacy—dispatched ambassadors to congratulate the pope on his arrival. At his residence beside the old Basilica of St. Peter, the pope received the men graciously, with no regard for past animosities. But still he only offered them the same terms as before. His demands: that every state pay an indemnity of more than a million florins to the apostolic treasury within four years, and that they virtually abandon all colleagues in the anti-papal alliance. The fact that Gregory hadn't softened his stance hamstrung any chance of achieving a quick resolution to the ill will.

And then an appalling event occurred that escalated hostilities to new heights.

All this time, war had been raging in the anti-papal city of Bologna north of Rome. Leading the papal forces there was the much-despised legate in that town, Cardinal Robert of Geneva. In the winter of 1376, he took his beleaguered troops to the town of Cesena, one of the last remaining strongholds of papal authority in the region, to rest and recuperate. The belligerent soldiers ran roughshod over the place, raiding homes and assaulting wives and daughters with abandon. By February 1, 1377, the citizens had had enough. They fought back, killing about 300 soldiers. The cardinal acknowledged his soldiers' misbehavior and promised a complete amnesty to Cesena so long as the people laid down their weapons and allowed him through the gates. The trusting people did so, but they were double-crossed. The vengeful cardinal and his men unleashed a three-day orgy of slaughter in Cesena. As men, women and children were murdered indiscriminately, the revenge-seeking cardinal was heard to ominously shout, "I will have more blood . . . kill all . . . blood, blood." Churches were also desecrated, and any churchman who tried to provide sanctuary to fugitives was murdered without hesitation. In the end, around 4,000 people died, many by drowning in the moat as they tried to escape. It's no wonder that, afterward, Robert was dubbed "the Butcher of Cesena."

As details of the incident spread throughout Italy, a collective cry of outrage rang out. Hearing of the horrors that were quickly assigned to soldiers acting on behalf of the church, the Florentines hardened their resolve to never trust the pope again. Catherine doesn't make any specific mention of the massacre at Cesena in her letters. But it must have weighed on her greatly when she wrote to Gregory a few weeks later: "Have mercy on so many souls and bodies that are perishing. O pastor and keeper of the cellar of the blood of the Lamb, don't allow trouble or shame or the abuse that you might be receiving draw you away, nor the perverse counselors of the devil who counsel you toward wars and miseries. Consider what great evils are resulting from this wicked war, and how great is the good that will be the result of peace."

Catherine told Gregory that it wasn't her intention to lecture him, but "I am compelled by gentle First Truth and by my desire, my dear *babbo*, to see you at peace, at rest, body and soul. For I don't see how, with these disastrous wars, you can have a single hour of good. What belongs to the poor is being eaten up to pay soldiers, who in turn devour people as if they were meat."

The pope's enduring affection for Catherine was made clear by three privileges he granted her. For one, she received the right to include three confessors in her entourage—usually Raymond, Bartolomeo Dominici and Giovanni Tantucci, a spiritual adviser and friend to William Flete. These confessors had been trained to hear confessions and give absolution and also to provide spiritual counsel when necessary, thus alleviating the burden placed on Catherine, who was attracting larger and larger crowds everywhere she went. For her chaplains, she also won for the right to celebrate "private" masses outside a chapel or church. These private masses had become necessary because of the amount of time she was spending on the road, where it wasn't always easy to find a church or chapel. And private masses ensured at least some level of privacy for those who didn't care for her public masses, which had become large, dramatic spectacles.

And still there was one more concession—one that was deeply gratifying for Catherine personally. For many years, she had dreamed of founding a women's monastery—not because she wanted to live there herself, but because she desired a home her female followers could share. In recent years she acted as a spiritual guide to women from all walks of life. But she wanted more for them. She wanted a beautiful space for them to live and worship together, one that was not closed to her, but where she could visit and lend an authoritative voice.

She had written the year before to Giovanni di Gano da Orvieto, an abbot she knew in the Orcia Valley, part of the agricultural hinterland of Siena, to ask for his help in locating "a suitable place for establishing a really good monastery." He turned to Nanni di Ser Vanni, once a monster of a man who changed his ways only after spending time with Catherine. Nanni was looking for a way to repay Catherine for her recent help in ending his involvement in a myriad of costly feuds. Upon learning of her request, he jumped into action. He decided to give her some of the land he owned just a few miles from Siena, on which stood the old Belcaro fortress, a twelfth-century building that enjoyed views so stunning they would one day inspire many a Renaissance painter. Nanni was only too happy to give the land to Catherine for free. At least part of the medieval fortress's structure was crumbling— the victim of battles between factions supporting the pope and the Holy Roman Emperor. But the foundation was in good shape, strong enough to hold a substantial structure. Indeed, it had all the makings of a wonderful gathering spot and was exactly the type of place Catherine was looking for.

The word "monastery" derives from the Greek word *monazein*, which means "to live alone." In Catherine's day, a monastery was a place where people could live out a fairly solitary life of prayer and reflection. The people who lived there were not necessarily nuns or monks, but religious men and women who desired to live apart from the rest of society.

To found a monastery, one needed the approval of both civil and religious authorities. The pope supplied the latter, but an additional clearance had to be secured from the leaders of Siena, who were understandably jittery about the idea of a privately owned fortress only three miles outside city walls. Catherine assured them that the site would not be used for military purposes and that it would only house religious women who would make prayers for them and the city of Siena part of their daily routine. On January 25, 1377, the city leaders voted in Catherine's favor, paving the way for Belcaro to become a monastery. Raymond wrote how all her spiritual sons and daughters pitched in to help transform what he called "a beautiful palazzo" into a monastery.

Eager to move ahead, Catherine's first course of action was to recruit women to live there, the first being Benedetta Salimbeni, the anxious daughter of the noble Salimbeni clan. The woman's husband had died, after which she suffered the death of her fiancé in a proposed second marriage. Now her family was pressuring her to marry a third time, mostly for political reasons. Catherine, who was acquainted with the young woman and her mother, wrote to Benedetta, telling her to consider the lamentable turn of events a sign that she should take Christ as her groom. Catherine told her that human husbands "pass away like the wine" and are often spiritually deadly for their wives. "You have experienced how constant they are, for in a short time the world has kicked you twice, and divine Goodness permitted this to make you run from the world," Catherine wrote. She begged the countess not to give in to the perverse temptations of society, but rather to run far from "the world's poison," no matter how handsomely packaged. She ended the letter by reporting great progress on her new monastery, adding, "If you come, you'll be coming to a land of promise!"

Catherine remained at Belcaro until late in April 1377, when she was asked to intervene in an especially bitter rivalry between two cousins of this same Salimbeni family residing in their respective castles about 30 miles south of Siena. While the roots of the disagreement between the cousins were petty—something having to do with a third castle they both wanted—their feud threatened the tranquility of the surrounding countryside and of her new monastery. Like many noble families of their day, the Salimbenis in their various branches retained private armies, and in no time even a trivial argument could snowball into serious fighting. On one side of the dispute was Cione di Sandro Salimbeni, a perpetual firebrand holed up in his fortress at Castiglioncello di Trinoro. (Cione had been one of those who tried to overthrow the Sienese government six years earlier, when Catherine stepped in to save her brothers from the hostile mob.) On the other side was Agnolino di Giovanni Salimbeni, who made his home at the Rocca d'Orcia, a dramatic tower of rock that rose from the floor of the Orcia Valley southeast of Siena.

At some point in this family squabble the Salimbeni women asked Catherine to step in as a mediator. Catherine was more than receptive to the idea; in her mind, the restoration of peace in the countryside epitomized her efforts to bring peace to Italy's embattled city-states. And so she and Raymond and a few others, including Lapa, Lisa Colombini and Tommaso della Fonte, took off on foot for Montepulciano, possibly pulling oxcarts filled with produce, and finally came to the home of Cione Salimbeni. We know only a few details of their negotiations, yet it seems that Cione's differences with his cousin quickly faded away in the warmth of her presence.

From there, Catherine went on and climbed up the dramatic hill of Rocca d'Orcia, with Agnolino Salimbeni's fortress perched on its top. Once there she presented herself and the general terms of Cione's offer to the family. To the younger cousin, they seemed entirely reasonable, and so the dispute that had been so intractable abruptly came to an end.

With the major goal of her mission already accomplished, Catherine was invited to move into the Salimbeni fortress, which was surrounded by beautiful gardens, as a guest of Agnolino and Monna Biancina, Agnolino's mother. But the move sparked resentment among Catherine's many friends and followers. Those at Belcaro had been under the impression that Catherine would be more personally involved in the day-to-day running of the monastery, so they were particularly unhappy about her long absences. In something of a terse response, Catherine informed them that her time away was actually beneficial to the women, since "good children do more when their mother is away than when she is there, because they want to show their love for her and get more into her good graces."

People back in Siena, which was suffering under conflict with the pope, were asking for her as well. Even nonpolitical citizens were frightened, as it had become all too easy to inadvertently raise suspicion. As in the case of the beheaded prisoner Niccolo di Toldo, a foolhardy word uttered to the wrong person could result in imprisonment, possibly even execution. Catherine was sympathetic, and she urged the Riformatori government to be more compassionate. Not only had scores of political prisoners been arrested on the thinnest of pretexts, but Siena's jails were already bursting at the seams with prisoners of war captured in battle against pro-pope forces. In March 1377, Catherine dictated a letter to the "prisoners of Siena," appealing to them to joyously accept their fate in the same way Christ accepted his on the cross.

Meanwhile, Gregory echoed the cries of others by calling for her presence in Rome. The pope felt weakened both physically and emotionally. Holed up in his palace, he was leery of citizens who were mostly strangers to him and of bishops and other churchmen who were still brooding over their departure from Avignon.

Despite all these pleas and concerns, Catherine stayed put.

There was something about her time spent with the Salimbenis that nurtured Catherine's soul. For one thing, the panoramic landscape was stunning. Gently rolling hills around the Orcia River were covered in vineyards, olive groves and beech and chestnut trees. Frequently painted by artists both during Catherine's time and now, the Val d'Orcia was dotted with stone houses on the tops of hills with cypress-lined roads leading up to them. Colors were vibrant, from the bright green grass of spring to the earth colors of summer. In addition, Catherine also was afforded plenty of time for prayer and personal reflection in the interludes when she wasn't preaching. When she did speak, large crowds materialized, seemingly from out of nowhere. She stayed more than four months in these parts, settling disagreements and negotiating peace among various factions and families. After so many setbacks with the Florentines, it must have been nice to experience some successes. At one point, she excitedly exclaimed that "so many demons are being eaten up that Tommaso [della Fonte] says he has a stomach ache." And there was more. Hearing that a miracle worker was in their midst, people in surrounding towns began bringing her their sick—and even those possessed by the devil.

Indeed, according to Raymond, it was during this time that Catherine found herself up against an evil spirit that had so completely overtaken a local woman that she had been forsaken by everyone in the region. At first, Catherine tried everything she could to evade the troubled woman. She was tired and had battled plenty of her own internal demons and so initially wanted no part of it, which was highly unusual. But it was nearly impossible to make oneself invisible inside the Salimbeni castle, and Monna Biancina had little trouble arranging an "accidental" meeting between the two women. As soon as Catherine came close to the woman, the spirit inside her howled. Catherine commanded it to leave the poor woman in peace, and the spirit immediately did just that, leaving its victim relieved but weary and with no memory of her ordeal.

While all this was going on, Raymond was hoping to placate at least some of those clamoring for Catherine by traveling to Rome in her place. But he was probably surprised when, once there, the pope ordered him to become the new prior of Santa Maria sopra Minerva, the main Dominican church in the city. As a result, he was not able to return to Siena or the Orcia Valley. The pope felt he was surrounded by people he couldn't trust and so would have wanted Raymond close by. That fall, Raymond had written Catherine to say that, contrary to their expectations, the pope's move to Rome had not ushered in any significant reforms in church management. The corruption and immorality of the papal court ran rampant in Rome, just as it did in Avignon. He also informed her that the pope was annoyed that she had still not joined him.

In turn, Catherine gave Raymond a message to pass on to Gregory: "Had you only . . . [begun church reforms] the very day you got back where you belong! I trust in God's goodness and in your holiness that you will do what had not yet been done . . . You know (for you were told) that is what you were asked to do: to see to the reform of holy Church; to attend to the punishment of sins and the planting of virtuous pastors; and to grasp the opportunity for holy peace with your wicked children in the best way possible and the manner most pleasing to God." His failure to make peace, she said, was a direct cause of so much "devastation and harm and disrespect [that] have befallen holy Church and her ministers." Although she admitted that she had disobeyed God by not staying close to the pope, she still didn't offer to come.

One reason Catherine wouldn't go to Rome was because of a new idea that had been percolating inside her. In a sense she had come to the end of a natural path of spiritual maturity, a path that had led her to this particular moment in time. Ever since she had left her solitary life in her cell, she had sought to better communicate the meditations and revelations born out of her years of intense prayer and communication with God. Catherine felt that all this, her absorption of divine truths, should be shared with the world. And so she knew what she would have to do. The illiterate woman would write a book.

NINE

Brilliant Work

Like so many other things in Catherine's life, the idea of writing a book was born in a vision. It was a Saturday in October 1377, and Catherine had gone to morning Mass following a night of deep prayer in her room. She walked up toward the altar and, without warning, fell to the floor, sliding into a trance—or a state of ecstasy—so intense she completely lost sight of the world around her. Without any prompting, she began reciting four prayers of petition, the first being for Catherine herself, that she might find God's truth. The second was for the reform of the church. The third was for the world in general. And the fourth was for the assurance of God's providence in all matters. These petitions, and the responses she received to them, form the crux of her book, which was eventually called *The Dialogue* because its contents are, indeed, a dialogue between Catherine and God. In it, she generally addresses God as "the father" and she typically refers to herself as "the daughter."

Raymond described the event like this: "So about two years before her death, such a clarity of Truth was revealed to her from heaven that Catherine was constrained to spread it abroad by means of writing, asking her secretaries to stand ready to take down whatever came from her mouth as soon as they noticed that she had gone into ecstasy. Thus in a short time was composed a certain book that contains a dialogue between a soul who asks the Lord four questions, and the Lord himself who replies to the soul, enlightening her with many useful truths."

Catherine ranks high among the great writers in church history, and her book *The Dialogue* is considered by many church experts a masterful treatise on spiritual growth. Other Catholic women writers have proven to be equally prodigious but only rarely have their epochal contributions made the same kind of enduring impact on the Catholic faith as Catherine's.

Largely because of the wisdom of their writings, Pope Paul VI named Catherine and Teresa of Ávila (from the sixteenth century) as Doctors of the Church in 1970, the first women to be awarded this rare and solemn distinction. This recognition marked a new chapter in the church's history and testifies to the respect accorded to their written interpretations of scripture. Since 1970, only two other women have been named doctors. In 1997, Thérèse of Lisieux, who lived in the nineteenth century, became the third woman given the title, followed in 2012 by Hildegard of Bingen, born in 1098. As of 2015, the church has bestowed this special recognition on only 36 people.

Hildegard, in particular, paved the way for Catherine and is perhaps the only woman before Catherine's time to make such an indelible mark on an established church that could not have been any more male dominated. The German mystic was in her early 40s when she heard a voice telling her to write down all the visions she had seen—and there were many. But the very thought of putting what she saw down on paper made her stomach queasy as there was no precedent for public female theologians. With some help, though, she eventually did write several works in Latin. Indeed, her first and most famous book was *Scivias*—or "Know the Ways"—containing 26 of the religious visions she experienced. In time, Hildegard's writings became extensive, encompassing theology, prophecy and medicine; she also wrote Europe's first morality play—accompanied by her own music.

Meanwhile, when it came to Thérèse, she displayed a writing style much like Catherine's—full of passionate and emotive rhetoric. Her autobiography, *Story of a Soul,* is one of the most widely read spiritual works ever, relaying her very simple take on spirituality: God is a loving God, and our response is only love.

In her book *Accidental Theologians*, Elizabeth A. Dreyer writes that the four female Doctors of the Church shared a bold and courageous spirit. "Medieval women could be imprisoned, tortured, or burned at the stake for transgressing established gender barriers of Church and society," she said.

Catherine may not have known how to read or write, but she was an indefatigable conversationalist, and her stream-of-consciousness exchanges with the Lord have made *The Dialogue* one of the most brilliant works in the history of the Catholic Church. Both instructive and profound, the book has been described by Sister Suzanne Noffke as a great tapestry to which Catherine adds stitch upon stitch until she is satisfied that she has communicated all she can of what she has learned about the ways of God. In fact, she chose to make God the central narrator—an acknowledgment of the way the missive spilled out of her as well as an act of careful deliberation on her part. Catherine knew that readers were less likely to pay heed to a message if they believed it to be from a simple uneducated woman. But if God spoke directly to them—if she could channel God's desires to them—then the message certainly would carry more weight.

The book begins with a remarkable passage on the essence of mysticism with Catherine as its focus: "A soul rises up, restless with tremendous desire for God's honor and the salvation of souls. She has for some time exercised herself in virtue and has become accustomed to dwelling in the cell of self-knowledge in order to know better God's goodness toward her, since upon knowledge follows love. And loving, she seeks to pursue truth and clothe herself in it." As always, self-knowledge is the bedrock on which Catherine builds her theology and spirituality.

However, contemplation in isolation was not the answer; Catherine herself eventually realized that she was bidden to bring her good works to the world. In another powerful section, Catherine warns of the dangers of selfishness and states God's desire that people be interdependent, sharing the unique gifts he has given to each of them with one another.

> I have distributed [all virtues and graces] in such a way that no one has all of them. Thus have I given you reason—necessity in fact—to practice mutual charity. For I could well have supplied each of you with all your needs, both spiritual and material. But I wanted to make you dependent on one another so that each of you would be my minister, dispensing the graces and gifts you have received from me. So whether you will it or not, you cannot escape the exercise of charity! Yet, unless you do it for love of me, it is worth nothing to you in the realm of grace. So you see, I have made you my ministers, setting you in different positions and in different ranks to exercise the virtue of charity. For there are many rooms in my house. All I want is love. In loving me you will

realize love for your neighbors, and if you love your neighbors you will have kept the law.

The Dialogue then homes in on the theme of Christ serving as our bridge to God, a bridge we can cross if only we renounce sin and know the Lord. In describing the bridge, God refers to three stairs, which represent the three stages of spiritual development. For Catherine, knowledge of God and knowledge of self go hand in hand in aiding our progression toward spiritual enlightenment. But to her this knowledge is not simply the result of an intellectual journey; it is rather the kind of knowledge that is fed through the loving affection of an abiding friendship.

Catherine's portrayal of the human person is also exceptional. God says to her that he made her soul in his own image, giving her memory, understanding and will: "The soul cannot live without love. She is always trying to love something because love is the stuff she is made of, and through love I created her. This is why I said that it is affection that moves the understanding, saying, as it were, 'I want to love, because the food I feed on is love.' And the understanding, feeling itself awakened by affection, gets up, as it were, and says, 'If you want to love, I will give you something good that you can love.' And at once it is aroused by the consideration of the soul's dignity and the indignity into which she has fallen through her own fault."

Legend has it that she completed the book in a single five-day state of ecstasy, between October 8 and October 13 in 1377. But most modern scholars believe it actually took her the better part of a year to complete it. Certainly she gave shape to much of the composition while staying in the Salimbeni fortress but added the finishing touches after returning to Siena, according to Raymond.

Either way, Tommaso Caffarini gives us an intriguing peek into the creative process behind *The Dialogue:*

> I say also that I have very often seen the virgin in Siena, especially after her return from Avignon, rapt beyond her senses, except for speech, by which she dictated to various writers in succession sometimes letters and sometimes the book, in different times and in different places, as circumstances allowed. Sometimes she did this with her hands crossed on her breast as she walked about the room; sometimes she was on her knees or in other postures; but always her face was lifted toward heaven. Concerning the composition of her book, then: This among other marvels occurred in the virgin: When emergencies would cause several days to pass in which she was kept from pursuing her dictation, as soon as she could take it up again she would begin at the point where she had left off as if there had been no interruption or space of time. Moreover, as is evident in the course of her book, sometimes after she had dictated several pages, she would summarize or recapitulate the main content as if the things she had dictated were (and in fact they were) actually present in her mind.

Catherine referred to the work—which was first published in the original Italian in 1472, many years after her death—simply as "my book" and later relegated its fate to Raymond in a document generally referred to as her "spiritual will": "I ask you also—you and brother Bartolomeo Dominici and brother Tommaso [della Fonte] and the maestro [Giovanni Tantucci]—to take in hand the book and any of my writings that you find. Together with master Tommaso [Pietra, another close disciple] do with them what you see would be most for the honor of God. I found some recreation in them."

Most scholars agree that the meaning of Catherine's writings—while insightful—can be difficult to disentangle. Many parts are wordy and repetitive; others include complex run-on sentences. Catherine herself seemed to recognize her deficiencies, and begged Raymond's forgiveness: "Pardon me for writing too much, but my hands and tongue go along with my heart!"

It was after she began work on *The Dialogue* that Catherine claims to have miraculously learned to write. The power seems to have suddenly come to her via some kind of spiritual intuition while she was staying at the Rocca d'Orcia in the fall of 1377. "This letter," she wrote to Raymond, "and another that I sent you, I have written with my own hand on the Isola della Rocca, with many sighs and an abundance of tears, so that the eye, though seeing, saw not. I was full of wonder at myself and at the goodness of God, considering his mercy towards the creatures that possess reason—and his providence, that so abounded towards me so that, for my refreshment, he gave me and prepared me to receive the faculty of writing so that I might have somewhere to relieve my heart. In a wonderful way, God set my mind to be able to do this, as the master does to the child when he shows him how to copy. As soon as you had left me, with the glorious evangelist John and Thomas of Aquinas, I began to learn in my sleep."

It's hard to know exactly how to consider such an audacious letter, so full of self-important pronouncements. Clearly Raymond didn't know what to make of it either. As with Catherine's description of the beheading of Niccolo di Toldo, Raymond never makes mention of this letter or the miracle of her learning to write in his biography. (The miracle was included in later hagiographical works, most notably the one by Tommaso di Antonio Nacci Caffarini.)

Continued discomfort with the idea that Catherine miraculously learned to write is evident in the failure of Karen Scott—an associate professor at Chicago's DePaul University who has written extensively about Catherine for Cambridge Journals and other publications—to acknowledge the existence of this letter to Raymond, let alone discuss its significance, in an essay specifically on the subject of Catherine as a writer of letters. "Writing for her was simply a form of speaking," Scott wrote, and it therefore makes no difference whether or not she actually was able to write for herself.

The French Dominican Père Hurtaud, who is among those who have edited editions of *The Dialogue*, has also expressed doubt about Catherine's precipitous ability to inscribe her own words, arguing that someone could have tampered with her letter to Raymond and that no letters written by Catherine herself have been preserved.

Whatever one thinks of that miracle, *The Dialogue* was and is Catherine's spiritual compendium: everything she had learned about the spiritual life, all bound together in one package. Oddly enough, a certain pessimism infuses her writing toward the end of *The Dialogue*. Catherine claimed to record God's own words when she wrote, "Sometimes I let the whole world be against the just, and in the end they die a death that leaves worldly people in wonder."

The days of late 1377 and early 1378 passed slowly, and there were many times when a weary Catherine didn't feel well enough to work on the book or anything else. She was dedicated, most certainly. But she was exhausted both mentally and physically, which made getting through the days a chore. And yet there was still so much more she had to accomplish.

Making matters worse was that, with Raymond in Rome, Catherine often felt horribly lonely, far from many of those she'd known and loved best. Despondent, she wrote him, "As for me, if it be [God's] will, let him take from me this dark life, for life is burdensome to me, and I long for death. Take heart, and let's be glad and joyful, because our happiness will be complete in heaven."

By this time, the year 1377, Catherine was 30 and the energetic young dyer's daughter of yore was nowhere to be found. Her personality was the same, her determination intact, but her appearance had changed dramatically. According to biographer Sigrid Undset, Catherine's body had become akin to a fragile, almost transparent vase, lit from within by her burning soul. In the past, not eating had perversely encouraged Catherine to work even harder. But by this time it was clear that her poor dietary habits had gone on for too long.

But although Catherine was a sickly woman (and one whose relationship with a mirror was nonexistent), it was just at this time, during her stay at Rocca d'Orcia, that she supposedly awakened a long-dead erotic passion in a man. Undset and others write of a young monk who became her disciple but was then consumed with the wrong kind of love for her. When Catherine failed to reciprocate his feelings, the man turned violent and desperate, so much so that one day in church he apparently tried to kill her. Those with Catherine managed to hold him back, and he fled, throwing off his monk's habit and later, according to some accounts, taking his own life. Two letters that Neri di Landoccio (who was a poet and one of her three secretaries during this period) received while he was at Rocca d'Orcia from someone who did not sign them—"for I do not know what my name is"—may have been from this man. The letters reveal someone who doesn't turn away from religion but who is simply losing the taste for those things that once made him glad to be alive. "I have been turned from the table because I have clothed myself in darkness . . . God in His mercy give you grace, perseverance and a holy death," he writes.

Catherine, who had prayed long and hard for God to save the lost disciple's soul, was probably privy to the news of his disappearance and perhaps even his suicide. But she never let on. There are only a few lines in a letter to Neri that might pertain to the incident: "Do not be afraid. God does not wish that the same should happen to you as to that other." Neri had always been a melancholy man, and perhaps he was ashamed of his dependence on Catherine. If the anonymous letters Neri received are from the monk who killed himself, he and Neri must have been familiar with one another.

Catherine, too, found herself heading into something of a depressing downward spiral. The pope may have been firmly ensconced in Rome, but tensions persisted. The intransigent Florentines had only dug in their heels, fueling more hostilities. Meanwhile, in Avignon, the cardinals who had stayed behind were still behaving shamelessly, with little regard for moral rectitude.

At this juncture, then, Catherine asked God what—besides her book—he would have her focus her energies on. The answer came in early 1378 when the pope ordered her to go to Florence once again in a renewed effort to broker peace. Even though negotiations had ruptured the previous October, and Florence remained obstinate in its disobedience, neither party had entirely abandoned hope of a compromise. With a dwindling amount of money in their coffers, the positions of both the papacy and the Florentines were no longer tenable. Gregory wrote to Raymond, "It has been written to me that if Catherine of Siena goes to Florence, I will have peace." Raymond dutifully replied that he was also willing to go to Florence. But Gregory demurred, saying, "I do not wish you to go because they would maltreat you, but I do not believe that they would harm Catherine, for she is a woman and they hold her in reverence." Raymond had no choice but to draw up the proper paperwork and dispatch it to Catherine, who immediately took off for Florence with a few of her followers.

The exact date of her arrival is uncertain, but it was no later than the beginning of March 1378 that Catherine found herself back in Florence. The pope was less interested in her appeals to the people than he was in her progress with the city's leaders, whom Gregory was desperate to win over. For once in Catherine's life, we have an external—and not entirely positive—corroboration of events. "It happened that there was in Florence a woman named Catherine," begins an account by Marchionne di Coppo Stefani, a Florentine historian and politician, "the daughter of Giacomo Benincasa, who was holy, pure and chaste, began to blame the opponents of the church. It is true that she knew ecclesiastical matters, both by her natural talents and by what she had acquired, and she spoke and wrote very well." Stefani goes on to say that Catherine was allowed many times to attend the meetings of the governing party, where she had no qualms about admonishing them for going against the pope. "She was reputed to be a prophetess by those in the Party, and by others, she was considered a hypocrite and a bad woman," he writes. "Many things were said about her, some about treachery, and others believed that they were speaking well by speaking evil of her."

In her dealings with the Florentines—or with anyone else for that matter—Catherine never held back. When writing of God's rebuke of religious people who lead extravagant lives, she said they were meant to be "fragrant flowers" in the larger garden of the church, but that they were instead like "stinking weeds full of impurity and avarice and bloated with pride."

With progress painfully slow, Catherine let her downheartedness show in a letter to one of her disciples in Siena, Nigi di Doccio Arzocchi, in which she wrote, "It is time to weep and sigh and pray for Christ's dear bride [the church] and for the whole Christian people, so afflicted because of our sins."

Even so, Catherine tried hard to buck up the spirits of Raymond, who, in Rome, was even more angst ridden. Reflecting on the church as an ark, she wrote:

> We must board the little ship of the most holy cross and fearlessly navigate this stormy sea. Those of us who are aboard this little ship have no reason for slavish fear, because the ship is provisioned with every food the soul can imagine. And if head winds blow that would beat against us and delay us so that we cannot fulfill our desires, we are not concerned. We stay there in living faith, because we have plenty to eat and the little ship is so strong that no wine, no matter how terrible, can dash it against the rocks and wreck it . . . So I beg you and I want you to board this little ship of the most holy cross, stripped of selfish love and clothed in the teaching of Christ crucified. Use it to navigate the stormy sea with the light of living faith and the pearl of true holy justice toward both yourself and those in your charge.

Meanwhile, the nearby town of Sarzana, located on the northern boundary of Tuscany, was chosen as the place to convene a peace conference. The Italian statesman Bernabò Visconti was picked to represent the anti-papal league. (Only the year before, 1377, he had craftily secured the loyalty of the famed mercenary John Hawkwood by giving him one of his illegitimate daughters, Donnina, in marriage.) Acting on the pope's behalf were a Benedictine cardinal and two other French prelates. The delegates made quick progress, easily settling on the amount of the indemnity—less than half of what the pope had originally demanded—and closing in on an agreement to other terms and conditions. But nothing had been finalized. And then, according to various accounts, everything changed. A knock came one evening at the Porta San Frediano, one of the doors to the city after it was walled in, and a thunderous cry could be heard: "Open quickly to the messenger of peace!" Holding their weapons, the guards opened the door but saw nobody there. Then a similar proclamation rang out from out of nowhere throughout the city: "The olive has come, the peace is made!" Believing a peace treaty had been secured, crowds of cheering people carrying torches spilled out of their homes and into the streets. The puzzled priors of Sarzana ordered everyone back to their homes, unaware of any reason to be celebrating. It was a few days later that the news finally reached Florence: Pope Gregory XI had died at the very hour of that knock on the door, on March 27, 1378. Some spooked citizens believed it might have been the pontiff's ghost, trying to pay one final visit to the city he'd grown tired of fighting.

Catherine and her disciples couldn't believe what they were hearing as no one had informed them that Gregory was even sick. If anything, they'd heard he was an active player in the peace talks. But apparently that wasn't the case, and the pope died a mere 14 months after parading triumphantly into Rome at the head of a joyful procession. Although the suddenness of his passing had caught Catherine off guard, it paled in comparison to her worries over selecting a successor. Like many in Italy, she feared a new pope could lead to the departure of the papacy—again—from Rome, especially with the French cardinals holding such significant sway. The citizens of Rome wasted no time in loudly demanding that an Italian—and preferably a Roman—be elected immediately. At least some of their representatives, always a disagreeable bunch, perniciously appealed to the fretful cardinals, warning that they might face death if an Italian wasn't chosen. Someone went so far as to tell Cardinal Jean de Cros to elect an Italian "or all the cardinals from beyond the Alps will be knifed." The possibility that the angry Romans might use violence to ensure their selection of a new pope was one possibility they did not want to face. But now it seemed that this was exactly what was happening.

Of the 16 cardinals who convened on April 7 to elect a new pope, 11 were French and they were, of course, leaning toward choosing one of their own. Their Italian counterparts also wanted a compatriot, with the fiery Roman populace seconding that opinion. Rattled by the Roman demonstrators chanting loudly in the streets outside their meeting, the nervous electors believed that picking an Italian was the only way to ward off widespread violence. After passing over Cardinal Giacomo Orsini, the Roman favorite, they finally settled on a compliant prelate named Bartolomeo Prignano, who was not a cardinal and therefore could not vote. Born in Naples in 1318, Prignano, archbishop of Bari, was a short, stout man who was thoroughly schooled on the administration of the church. Known as an enemy of extravagance, he was respected for his integrity, having faithfully served Gregory as vice chancellor both in Avignon and in Rome. Moreover, he was not tied to any political faction, and he enjoyed amicable relations with both the Italians and the French.

Feeling certain the election had already happened, an unruly mob burst into the conclave with demands they be presented with the new pope. Amid considerable confusion, the frightened cardinals suddenly regretted their decision to opt against a Roman. Thinking fast on their feet, they resorted to a ruse. They quickly dressed up an elderly Roman cardinal named Francesco

Tebaldeschi in pontifical robes and paraded him out before the people in an attempt to pacify them. Satisfied with the choice, the crowd dispersed. But then, without further ado, it was Prignano's election that was formally announced. He took the name Urban VI and was crowned in Rome. Despite the misgivings of some, the fact that the new pope's election took place in Rome—the first time that had happened in 75 years—immediately brightened the political landscape. Trading goodwill gestures, the Florentines promised to abide by the papal interdict until peace negotiations were finalized, while Urban renewed the truce that Gregory had sanctioned while talks were ongoing.

Urban's penchant for frugality and integrity initially raised Catherine's hopes for reformation. "It seems to me the dawn is beginning to break just a little bit," she wrote to William Flete. "I mean our Savior has enlightened this people to let them be roused from the perverse blindness in which they have sinned by using force to have [the liturgy] celebrated. Now, by divine grace, they are observing the interdict and beginning to turn toward obedience to their father."

But it didn't take long for her to doubt whether the new pope was all that he seemed on the surface. Urban may have been committed to church reform, but his arrogant approach to tackling it quickly alienated many of his cardinals. Indeed, his surprising election and sudden rise to the top of the church hierarchy served to have stripped him of all humility—and perhaps even affected his brain. The way he rudely enforced his will was intensely galling to his curia, accustomed to being treated with respect and dignity. Abandoning all pretense of decorum, Urban point blank branded Cardinal Orsini, who was a member of a distinguished Roman family, a "complete fool." On another occasion, he rushed at the Cardinal de Cros in an attempt to strike

him after becoming irritated by something he had said. The new
pope had to be physically restrained from pummeling him. The
cardinals had thought he'd be an amenable figurehead, grateful to
be thrust from insignificance to power. Instead, he took his new
role seriously, chastising the French cardinals for their immorality and threatening to pack the Sacred College with Italians.
The threat alarmed not only King Charles V of France, but even
Queen Giovanna from his native Naples. Soon Urban VI, who
was proving to be deranged, stood almost ally-less in his unwarranted indignation.

But Catherine was forever loyal to the pope, no matter what
his transgressions. As Suzanne Noffke put it, Catherine "continued to support Urban VI simply because she was convinced
that he was the legitimately elected pope and therefore was to be
obeyed even if he were the devil incarnate."

Catherine wrote to Cardinal Peter de Luna, who was waver-
ing in his support for Urban, to urge his continued allegiance. She
acknowledged hearing that "discord is arising in Rome between
Christ on earth [the pope] and his disciples. This causes me un-
bearable sorrow . . . Tell the pope to provide himself with good
pillars, now that he is about to appoint some cardinals. Stop wasting time! Don't wait so long to do what is needed, or the stones
will be falling on our heads!"

She also dictated a plea to him, asking that he do whatever
was necessary for God's honor and the reform of the church, "and
to eliminate this scandal."

She intimated her fear of a Western Schism, discussed openly
among the disaffected cardinals just months after Urban's election. Although Gregory died in Rome, many of his cardinals were
still in Avignon. Indeed, there were enough cardinals in both

Rome and Avignon—all of whom would have done anything to retain their privileges—to create two bases of power.

They began whispering that perhaps Urban's election was illegitimate. After all, the threat of violence had put undue pressure on them. The whole matter distressed Catherine greatly, especially since there was nothing she could do about it. From Florence, she was rendered impotent, unable to muzzle those scheming against Urban in Anagni, the hill town near Rome that had been Pope Gregory's summer residence. Her main secretary, Stefano Maconi, had returned to Siena and was replaced by the loyal Barduccio di Piero Canigiani, the youngest son of her Florentine benefactor who would become a vital part of Catherine's inner circle. Now she wrote to Stefano and asked him to secure the manuscript she had left behind at Rocca d'Orcia. At least she could rely on the natural rhythms of daily work on the book to provide a distraction.

Yet scarcely had she returned to her dictations when unrest broke out again in a city that appeared incapable of keeping a lid on instability. The continued embargo on Florentine goods had finally forced old hostilities among the many political factions to the surface. Economically strapped, the lower classes demanded a more equitable fiscal policy in a series of petitions presented to Florence's executive council. The disenfranchised then took out their anger on the rich, looting shops and homes, including one that belonged to Niccolo Soderini. The patriotic political figure was one of those who had gone to Siena and begged Catherine to come to Florence in the first place. Armed crowds protested in the streets, chanting and marching over the medieval stone Ponte Vecchio bridge toward the south bank of the Arno River. Once there, someone in the group remembered that Catherine, now referred to as the "witch," was staying nearby, close to the bottom of the San Giorgia hill.

Catherine heard them coming. Her disciples had known about the growing unrest for days and had urged her to flee, but she refused. Now she and her friends assembled in her garden and listened as the cries of the mob grew louder.

TEN

A Turn for the Worse

As the crowd's cries grew louder and more boisterous, Catherine and her friends prayed to themselves. Mustering all her strength, she asked God to keep those who were with her safe. She didn't care about herself. The menacing wall of people pressed closer until they were just outside the gate. Without knowing their exact motive, Catherine's followers stayed silent, not sure how to react. But Catherine was sure, or at least was hoping, that they were coming for her. And when they finally moved in, brandishing swords and spears, they were indeed calling for her head.

Raymond wasn't there, but he heard all about the incident later. He described the scene: While Catherine and her followers were praying in the garden, the rioters, the "satellites of Satan," came with weapons, shouting, "Where is that wicked woman? Where is she?" Raymond said that when Catherine heard this, she steeled herself mentally for the martyrdom she had so long desired. She stepped directly in front of a man who was carrying a sword and crying out louder than the rest, and said, "I am Catherine. Do with me whatever our Lord may permit, but in the name of the Almighty I command you to harm none of my companions." At that, Raymond said, the rioters were so disconcerted that they seemed unable to move, much less strike a blow at her. They turned around and left.

Although other accounts of the event describe the weapon as a dagger and Catherine as standing rather than kneeling, the essence of what happened is clear. A mob of angry men wanted to kill Catherine. But she actually hoped to die a martyr and said to them, "If you mean to kill me, do so. I shall not resist." The mob had no idea how to respond to such a statement. Catherine's companions were relieved, but not Catherine. She cried out in sadness, saying, "Oh what a disappointment . . . I thought that he who in his mercy granted me the white rose of virginity would grant me also the red rose of martyrdom. But alas, no! . . . This is the result of my innumerable sins."

Just after the confrontation with the mob, Catherine emphasized yet again her desire to die as a martyr in a letter to Raymond. "My heart almost burst with the desire to give my life, and this desire was both sweet and painful—sweet because I had become one with the Truth, painful because it tore my heart to see this insult to God and this crowd of demons which darkened the sky and blinded men's understanding, for it seemed as though God let them do as they wanted for the sake of justice and vengeance. I sighed because I was afraid for the misfortune this would be if it became an obstacle in the making of peace."

Although she had escaped harm's way this time, Catherine realized that—for her followers' sake—it was probably best to leave the city. But the pope wouldn't hear of it. So she gathered her group together and moved them secretly into the home of a tailor and friend named Francesco di Pipino—one of the few people in the city who would have them. From all accounts, no one else came after them, but Florence as a whole experienced continuing bursts of unrest. For those in the city in the summer of 1378, a sequence of conspiracies and counter-conspiracies wreaked havoc and made it nearly impossible for Catherine to concentrate on matters of substance. Years after the Black Death had left a path of destruction in its wake, a different kind of plague struck—one created by a working class that had finally had its fill of gross social inequities.

By the fourteenth century, the production and sale of woolen cloth had made Florence a fairly prosperous city, but the divide between the lower classes and the wealthy had been accentuated. In addition, the city's war with the papacy that had begun in 1375 meant an increase in public expenditures—and then an increase in taxes. Faring poorly were the *ciompi*, or those workers who had the tedious task of carding or combing out the wool into manageable strands prior to weaving. They ranked so far down in Florentine society that even the weavers for the wholesale wool merchants were considered superior. Due to their propensity for radical behavior, the government had never allowed the *ciompi* to form their own guild, unlike almost all other craftsmen. Shut out of political life, these lower-class workers had fewer rights than other laborers and were subject to more controls. They had no say in the running of the government. As a result, they grew increasingly frustrated. Finally, in the summer of 1378, all their grievances with the system bubbled to the surface and then poured out. The *ciompi* and other lower-class workers who had been locked out of the political system, and on whose labor Florence's prosperity depended, took to the streets, rioting.

For a few weeks it seemed as though everyone in Florence was either making demands in the streets or taking cover inside their homes. The tipping point came when the enraged unguilded wool workers took up arms and attacked the Palazzo della Signoria, the town hall, calling for more equitable fiscal policies and the right to form a guild. The obstinate government refused to budge. Finally, on July 22, the people forced their way into the fortress-like palace and took control of the government council room and its occupants. The lower classes proclaimed the creation of a new, more socially representative government, installed a wool carder named Michele di Lando in the executive office and hung their flag outside the palazzo. They ordered the creation of new guilds so that the *ciompi* might finally have access to the political system. But soon the new regime was clashing with members of the traditional guilds, led by the guild of butchers.

In the end, the Ciompi Revolt of 1378, which traumatized members of Florence's upper classes for years to come, was a briefly successful insurrection of the disenfranchised lower classes that wanted a greater say in government. Today the revolt is sometimes referred to as the first industrial labor uprising in history.

Even with all that was going on around her, Catherine somehow remained fixated on the papacy. In her first letter to Urban VI that summer, she urged him to act with kindness but did not go so far as to mention his erratic behavior directly. She also expressed her support for the pope's campaign against the buying and selling of church offices and privileges. "Oh, wretched me," she wrote, "I say it sorrowfully! Your sons are feeding on what they receive through their ministry of the blood of Christ, and they aren't ashamed to act like gamblers, playing their games with those holy hands anointed by you, Christ's vicar! And that's saying nothing of all the other wretched things they are doing! . . . My dear *babbo*! Bring us a remedy!"

To Catherine, the church was a divine institution, and the pope was someone with divinely instituted power. Even if she didn't always agree with Urban, a break with him would have meant a break with Christ's vicar on earth. In addition, Urban was the first Italian pope in more than seven decades. Catherine would have done anything to help support him.

"Catherine's support for Urban was because she believed so strongly in the unity of the Church and that the pope is vicar of Christ, in spite of his limitations," said Mary Catherine Hilkert, O.P., a professor of theology at Notre Dame University.

Just days after the workers' revolt, progress was being made on another front. Three months after his election, Urban finally reached a peace treaty with the Florentines on July 28, 1378. Thanks to talks that had continued in Tivoli, near Rome, Florence was to pay the pope 200,000 florins (as opposed to Pope Gregory's original requirement of 1,000,000 florins). Florence was also to repeal all laws placed against the church and to restore all property confiscated or looted from the clergy. In return, Urban agreed to rescind the interdict and return Florence to the favor of the ecclesiastical community. Catherine couldn't have been happier, as is evident in this letter to a disciple in Siena: "Oh dearest children, the lame are walking, the deaf hear, the eyes of the blind see, and the mute speak, shouting with a loud voice: 'Peace! Peace! Peace!' They cry out with great joy at the sight of these children returning to obedience and their father's favor, their spirits reconciled."

With the peace deal signed and sealed, Catherine's presence was no longer required in Florence. In other circumstances, she might have stayed to celebrate the peace treaty with her friends there a while longer. But some in Florence were still suspicious of her motives, so she decided to leave sooner rather than later.

Catherine made plans to head back to Siena; she hadn't been there for more than five months. Although Catherine rarely wrote about the specifics of her trips, it must have taken her and her group many days to trek the 50 or so miles between Florence and Siena, traveling by foot and donkey. Along the way, they would have found sympathetic residents to host them and used the occasion of each stop to pray, comfort the sick and provide spiritual counseling.

Comfortably ensconced back home, she wrote a letter to the government leaders in Florence and apologized for leaving so abruptly. "I had wanted to leave and go back to Siena [only] after having celebrated and thanked divine Goodness and you," she said, "but now it seems the devil has so unjustly sown hostility toward me in [people's] hearts . . . But I go sad and dejected, leaving the city in so much bitterness."

In the letter, she told Florentine leaders exactly what she thought about the working-class struggle for reform: "You want to reform your city, but I'm telling you this desire will never be realized unless you do your best to demolish the hatred and rancor in your hearts and your self-centeredness. In other words, don't be concerned just for yourselves but for the general good of the whole city. So I'm begging you for the love of Christ crucified, for your own good, not to play favorites in choosing officials for your city but to choose virtuous men, wise and discerning, who with the light of reason will establish the order the city needs."

Back in familiar surroundings, Catherine for once put aside her preoccupation with politics and, after completing her book, lavished her counsel on friends and family members. She wrote a series of letters filled with spiritual advice, with not a word about church matters. And that was in spite of the storm clouds that were gathering over the papacy at this time. It's not clear what, if anything, she knew of a meeting held in August 1378 in Anagni, an ancient town in central Italy. At that meeting, 13 of the 16 cardinals who had elected Pope Urban VI the previous April solemnly decided to seek his abdication. Only the three Italian cardinals declined to take part. Although the legitimacy of the proceedings had not come into question at the time, the cardinals were by August so concerned about Urban's bizarre behavior that they claimed the election had been conducted under duress and that it was therefore null and void. At the Mass that was sung, even the priest's sermon weighed in favor of the cardinals' position: "The sheep of Christ's pasture are wandering through steep and devious ways, even as flocks that have no shepherd; he who usurpeth the name of shepherd, is not the shepherd, for he has not entered by the door into the sheepfold; he whose own the sheep are not, careth not to guard them from the invading wolves, from the roaring lions that are seeking to devour."

The cardinals stepped up their rhetoric in a follow-up document in which they called Urban an "Anti-Christ, devil, apostate, tyrant, deceiver, elected-by-force." After paying homage to this man for months, they now feared that they had been poor judges of character. Indeed, his treatment of cardinals had been so abusive, they believed he might be completely mad. They had never really wanted to elect him anyway, they reasoned, and had done so only out of fear for their lives. After a lengthy discussion, the cardinals elected Robert, the French cardinal of Geneva, as Pope Clement VII on September 20, 1378. Once the papal legate in Italy, Robert was the much-despised military leader who had calmed the rebellion at Cesena by authorizing the slaughter of thousands of people. He was enthroned on September 21 and crowned on October 31.

And thus began the Great Western Schism—driven by politics and Urban's instability—that split Western Christianity for four decades.

This divide placed the whole Western Christian world into opposing camps, creating a split in loyalties that ripped Europe apart. Lining up behind Urban was much of Italy, England, Poland and Hungary, while France, Scotland, Portugal, Naples and the Spanish kingdoms backed Clement. Even the saints clashed on the issue. Catherine wrote to Urban, "Those devils in human form have made an election. They have not elected a vicar of Christ, but an anti-Christ." But Vincent Ferrer, a Dominican priest ordained in 1378 who would be canonized in 1455, was convinced that the election of Urban was in question and tried to shore up Spanish support behind Clement. (Also supporting Clement was St. Colette.) It is a sign of just how complex the issue was that two of the church's most beloved saints, both renowned for their spiritual acumen, were at odds.

Catherine wrote of her anger to the three Italian cardinals: "You know the truth, that Pope Urban is indeed Pope, Supreme Pontiff, elected by regular election, not out of fear, in fact more by divine inspiration than through your human contrivances. This is what you proclaimed to us, and this is the truth. Now you have turned away like vile and miserable knights: your very shadow has frightened you."

In this crisis of authority, neither pope gained a decisive edge—at least not immediately. The schism was the most serious sociological disruption to impact the church to that point. The schism not only created two popes and two accompanying papal structures, but also sowed mass administrative and spiritual confusion as countries and leaders were forced to figure out which pope and papal system they wanted to acknowledge and follow.

Everywhere the faithful struggled with the question of who was the true pope. If that wasn't bad enough, the financial situation of the church as a whole grew even more precarious than it had been during the Avignon papacy. There were now two papal bases of power for which it was necessary to provide upkeep; there were two sets of cardinals entrenched in their power and privileges. When the two papal rivals began playing a game of one-upmanship in matters of pomp and patronage, resources evaporated even faster.

After hearing about Clement's election, Catherine wrote to Urban "with the desire of seeing you robed in the strong garment of most ardent charity, in order that the blows that are hurled at you by the wicked men of the world, lovers of themselves, may not be able to harm you." She told Urban to fight back courageously against the anti-Christ that the incarnate demons had created to work against him. She also warned him to look out for attempts against his life and called him "the cellarer who holds the keys to the wine cellar of holy Church in which is the blood of the humble spotless Lamb." She added that she would not be satisfied "until I speak with your holiness in person."

Urban was so rattled that he suddenly decided he absolutely had to have Catherine with him in Rome and ordered Raymond to make the arrangements. But Catherine insisted this time on a written order from Urban, not just a simple invitation. Her friends and family members had grown tired of her constant comings and goings, as had many of her sisters among the Mantellate. More than anything, they wanted her to be with them. Once Catherine obtained that order, though, she was determined to go. Accompanying her would be nearly 40 trusted friends, as well as a number of priests. Lapa, who was now about 71, was to remain in Siena, but Catherine arranged for her to follow once she had secured accommodations for them in Rome.

It took weeks for Catherine and her followers to complete their travel plans. In a late October letter to Francesco di Pipino, the Florentine tailor, Catherine said the exact route they would take was still being worked out. On November 4 she wrote him again with more specifics: "I'll be going to Rome from here about the middle of this month, more or less, as God pleases." In the end the dozens of people, both men and women, who joined her on the trip included her good friend Alessia Saracini, her follower Bartolomeo Dominici and her sister-in-law, Lisa Colombini. Finally, in November, they took off, passing through the Porta Romana, the Roman gate—one of 38 portals leading through the city's medieval walls—finally headed to Rome. Along the way, they acted like pilgrims, dividing up daily duties and seeking meals (everyone but Catherine, that is) wherever they could get them.

Catherine and her followers finally arrived in Rome on November 28, the first Sunday of Advent. The city they walked into was only a shadow of its former self, nothing like the cultural and educational powerhouse of the Mediterranean world it had been under Julius Caesar. The collapse of the empire and the unrest of the Middle Ages had almost decimated the once-great capital. With its population reduced to about 20,000 people, the ruins of ancient Rome were being used as pastureland—and picked apart for building material—by the time Catherine set eyes upon them. Rome was also a city of great violence, so frightening that for a brief period Urban was forced to hole up inside the Basilica of Santa Maria in Trastevere, the first church in Rome dedicated to the Virgin Mary, located about a mile from the Vatican.

During her time there, Catherine came upon many lovely centuries-old churches, but not the immense St. Peter's Basilica we know today. Construction on that church, the most famous

Roman Catholic church in the world, wouldn't begin until 1506. What Catherine saw was the original basilica, built starting in the fourth century atop an ancient burial ground that included what was believed to be the tomb of St. Peter. Unlike today, popes in the Middle Ages lived principally at the Lateran Palace across Rome, not at the basilica. By the time Gregory returned to Rome in 1377, the Lateran Palace had burned and the Vatican was—for the first time—used as a papal residence. But the compound was in shambles. The Vatican was in such a deplorable state that animals dug for bodies in the cemetery while cows grazed inside the basilica.

The joyful pope received Catherine on her second day there. Their only other previous meeting had been when Catherine visited Avignon. So comfortable was he with her that he didn't hesitate to immediately beg a favor: Would she make a speech to the assembled cardinals, with the schism as its theme? She didn't hesitate. Of course she would. And she did so in a deeply affecting way. She urged the men to stay strong and explained in detail the reasons that courage was, particularly at this time, so important. She said God's providence watched over each person in a special way in times of crisis. They should not allow themselves to be frightened by the schism, she advised; they should persevere and work on God's behalf with no regard for men. When she finished her talk, the pope seemed genuinely appreciative. He summed up what she had said and added to the cardinals: "See, brothers, how guilty we must appear to God because we are without courage. This little woman puts us to shame. And when I call her a little woman I do not do so out of scorn, but because her sex is by nature fearful; but see how we tremble while she is strong and calm, and see how she consoles us with her words." With this, he gave Catherine and her followers his blessing.

A few days later, Urban asked something even more important of Catherine: he wanted her to travel to the kingdom of Naples, which comprised the southern part of the Italian Peninsula, to pay a personal call on Queen Giovanna.

On November 22, 1378, just a few days before Catherine arrived in Rome, Queen Giovanna had announced formally that she was throwing her considerable influence behind the new pope, meaning that her annual Neapolitan contribution of 64,000 florins would be going to Clement as well. The money part, in particular, stung. In retaliation, Urban published a long list of those officially branded as enemies of the church. The queen's name wasn't on it, but at the top was her pope—Robert of Geneva—as well as several members of her court. In what was becoming a real tit-for-tat, Giovanna then began replacing all of Urban's church officials in Naples with those sympathetic to Clement. Giovanna's moves wound up backfiring, though, as most of her people favored an Italian pope—a countryman—over a French one, even if the Italian one was a bit unstable.

Although the pope and Catherine were both swept up by the possibilities of what might be accomplished, Raymond apparently had reservations about the idea of sending Catherine to Naples, fearing the trip might place her in danger. But he stayed silent. As they discussed it, Urban suggested that another woman join Catherine on the mission. Karin, one of Bridget of Sweden's eight children (who would go on to become St. Catherine of Sweden), was in Rome at the time and was already familiar with Giovanna. Born in 1331, Karin was 16 years older than Catherine and extremely holy. When she was only 14, she married Eggard von Kurnen, but because she was so committed to God, she persuaded her new husband to join her in a vow of chastity. Catherine agreed to hold off on making any firm plans until the pope had consulted with Karin.

Catherine was excited, energized even, at the prospect of the Naples trip. A few days later, though, the whole plan began to unravel when Karin effectively nixed the idea, fearing it would be too risky. It didn't help that Karin thought very little of Giovanna, as the queen had apparently once used her feminine charms on Karin's brother, Karl, ultimately bringing about his moral disgrace. Of course, all this was good news for Raymond, who used the rejection as an opening to express his own reservations. Raymond had grown up 25 miles north of Naples and was all too familiar with Giovanna's court, where the occasional strangling wasn't uncommon.

Urban listened carefully to Raymond's concerns and finally agreed to cancel the trip. Catherine was annoyed at both of them. If she wasn't concerned about her personal safety, why should they be? "If Saint Agnes and Saint Margaret [two early Christian martyrs] had reasoned as you do, they would never have won the martyr's crown," she told Raymond. "Your reasonings are worthless; they come from your lack of faith and not from the genuine virtue of prudence." Nonetheless, Raymond and his objections prevailed.

Beside herself, Catherine dictated a letter to Queen Giovanna. "Dearest mother in Christ gentle Jesus," she began. "I Caterina, servant and slave of the servants of Jesus Christ, am writing to you in his precious blood. I long to see you grounded in truth, the truth we need to know and love in order to be saved." She reprimanded the queen for switching her loyalties, saying that she was behaving like one "who is the prey of passion." She also spelled out her case for Urban's legitimacy: "Return to the obedience of holy Church. Acknowledge the evil you have done. Humble your-self under the mighty hand of God, and God, who considers his servant's humility, will be merciful to us . . . I long for your salva-tion, and . . . I long to see you grounded in truth, because it is the truth that sets us free . . . I would much rather tell you the truth in person than in writing, for your own good and most of all for God's honor . . . I'll say no more. Keep living in God's holy and tender love."

However, despite Catherine's best efforts, Giovanna failed to join the Urban camp.

During the final months of 1378, Catherine suffered another personal setback. Out of the blue, Urban appointed Raymond—her closest friend and confidant—a papal legate and ordered him to visit Charles V in France so that he might plead the pope's case. Raymond went to her to break the news. She didn't want to lose him but agreed that Raymond had to go if it was what the pope wished. A few days before he was scheduled to leave, they met to reflect on the evolution of their friendship. In those days, women mystics were supposed to live under the continual guidance of a spiritual director to ensure that their mystical experiences con-formed to church precepts. Catherine must have wondered how she would get along without him. As Raymond remembered their meeting, "all other persons except the two of us were excluded—not that others were not present, but that they were not included in the conversation." When they were finished talking, Catherine said, "Go now with God, for I feel that never again in this life will we have a long talk together like this."

Now nearly 50 years old, Raymond was to sail in December from the old Roman port of Ostia, some 20 miles away, at the mouth of the Tiber River. On the day of his departure, Catherine and Raymond walked together to the docks. When Raymond's ship pulled away, he recalled seeing her kneeling down at the water's edge, weeping as she made the sign of the cross with her hand, again and again. Perhaps she believed that this was the last time she would see her beloved friend.

Catherine returned to Rome and embarked on the final chapter of her life feeling very much alone. She wrote a letter that she hoped Raymond would receive during a stopover in Pisa, encouraging him—as always—to do everything in his power to fulfill the pope's wishes. She knew that his was an arduous journey, the ship traversing challenging winter seas, but, as Catherine noted, Raymond had the truth to guide him: "We have seen in the light that our gentle God finds pleasure in few words and many deeds. Without the light we wouldn't have known this and therefore would have done just the opposite, speaking much and doing little. Our heart would be sailing on the wind, for in happy times we would be frivolous and unduly self-confident, and in time of sorrow inordinately sad."

She tried not to sound so morose and closed by saying, "And now, my soul, be silent and speak no more! I don't want to begin, dearest father, to say what I could neither write with pen nor speak in words. Let my silence tell you what I want to say."

Meanwhile, Urban was proving to be the young uneducated woman's loyal mentee, despite being unstable and power hungry. He always heeded her advice and never turned against her or became sulky as Gregory had whenever such advice caused him problems. The headstrong old pope seems never to have taken offense at anything she wrote to him. He showered fatherly affection on "this little woman" and revered her as the true and chosen spokesman of the Lord.

Tensions continued to flare between the dueling popes. On November 29, Urban excommunicated Cardinal Robert of

Geneva, a man separated from him by a mere 60 miles. He also excommunicated a number of other cardinals, prelates and princes who supported Robert, as well as the military leaders and troops the rival pope had amassed in the hopes of taking control of Rome and ousting Urban. He did not, however, excommunicate the three Italian cardinals, as he still hoped he might persuade them to come over to his side. Not long after, Clement got his revenge by creating six new cardinals loyal to him.

Christmas was coming—perhaps Catherine's first outside Siena. She sent the pope a lovely present, five oranges she had candied and covered with gold leaf. The gift was accompanied by a message. She told him that she was "desiring to free you from the bitter agony which rages in your soul. It is the pain which springs from the love of God—I mean the sorrow and pain caused by our own faults." Although Catherine was undoubtedly missing Raymond, her mother by this time had come down from Siena, which brought her some comfort.

For Urban, the year 1379 got off to a promising start when England declared itself emphatically behind the Roman claimant. King Louis of Hungary, who also believed Urban to be the true pope, promised assistance, going so far as to support armed intervention. In Catherine's hometown of Siena, the government had announced its unabashed approval of Urban.

But the three Italian cardinals still had not completely committed themselves to Urban or to Clement. The two papal claimants continued to recognize them as members of the Sacred College while the cardinals continued to address both Urban and Clement as the one lawful pontiff. In the second half of January 1379, the cardinals appear to have been doing a bit of a tightrope act, finally breaking off negotiations with Urban while still refusing to formally throw their support behind Clement. From Rome, an exasperated Catherine sent them a fiery rebuke: "O how mad you are, to have given the truth to us and preferred to taste the lie for yourselves." She called them "fools worth of a thousand deaths."

Unrest in the Catholic Church was about to grow a lot worse, and Catherine would have to step in.

ELEVEN

Spiritual Anxieties

If there was ever a time when Catherine displayed her commitment to peace, prayer and justice, it was the 17 months she spent in Rome during 1379 and 1380. Not only did she continue sending letters to anyone in need of spiritual guidance, she also focused on what she did best: pray. When it came to her dictations, it was prayer that took center stage. Some of these prayers were included in *The Dialogue*. Others, though, were gathered together after her death and eventually published as *The Prayers of Catherine of Siena*. Often they are long and dramatic, sometimes filling several pages. But a few are quite short and concise, consisting of only a few lines, such as this one: "O holy Spirit, come into my heart. By Thy power draw it to Thee, its God, and grant me love with fear. Guard me, Christ, from every evil thought. Warm me and enflame with Thy most sweet love, so that every pain may seem light to me. My holy Father and my sweet Master, help me now in all my ministry. Christ Love, Christ Love, Amen."

Taken together, they provide a window into the profound level of spiritual maturity she had reached by age 32. In total, 26 of her prayers have been preserved, all of which were recorded during the last four years of her life. For the most part, these are not prayers that she herself wrote or even formally dictated to others, but rather her actual prayers to God that were taken down as she uttered them by whichever secretary happened to be present. They are notable for their passion, their simplicity and their relentless desire for the salvation of others.

One of her most famous prayers was written in February 1379:

> In your nature,
>
> eternal Godhead,
>
> I shall come to know my nature.
>
> And what is my nature, boundless love?
>
> It is fire,
>
> because you are nothing but a fire of love.
>
> And you have given human kind a share in this nature,
>
> for by the fire of love
>
> you created us.
>
> And so with all other people
>
> and every created thing:
>
> you made them out of love.

Catherine's support of Pope Urban and her push for reforms and efforts to end the schism continued to be first and foremost in her mind, as is evident in this prayer from December 1378:

> And then, director of our salvation,
>
> let this new spouse of the Church [Urban]
>
> be directed always by your counsel.
>
> Let him accept

and listen to

and encourage

only those who are clean and pure.

As for these other newest plants of yours [the cardinals],

Let them stand before our lord your vicar on earth

just as the angels stand before you in heaven,

for the reform of this holy mother Church.

A month later, on the feast of the Chair of St. Peter in January 1379—a day commemorating Christ's choosing of Peter to sit in his place as the authority over the church—she prayed for the pope:

So [God] listen to us

as we pray for the guardian of this chair of yours,

whose feast we are celebrating.

Make your vicar

whatever sort of successor you would have him be

to your dear elder Peter,

and give him what is needed for your Church.

I am the witness

that you have promised to grant my desires soon;

With even more confidence then

I beg you to wait no longer

to fulfill these promises. O my God.

Catherine may have prayed beautifully and ceaselessly, but it wasn't enough to heal the divide. Although the schism crisis rose directly out of the recent double pontifical election, its roots ran deep, the natural result of decades-long tensions between French and Italian segments of the church following the Avignon papacy.

As Louis Salembier wrote in his Catholic history of the conflict published in 1907, "All the past trials of the Church appear to revive, all her future crises exist in embryo in this unfortunate schism." Catherine wished that she had more to show for her time in Rome. But Raymond was now in Genoa—having turned back from France after learning of a plot against his life—and she had no other spiritual adviser to turn to who was familiar with the inner workings of the papal court.

What is clear in all her writings is that Catherine's language was very much a reflection of her own passionate personality. As Sister Mary O'Driscoll, a leading authority on Catherine, puts it: "This is particularly evident in the anthropomorphic terms she uses to speak of God. Her God is 'mad with love' and 'drunk with love,' and acts 'as if he cannot live without us.' While her anthropomorphism, like her imagery, is a testimony to the inadequacy of human language to speak about the divine, it is also an expression of her own lively faith in a personal God, full of love and mercy."

As Catherine wasn't formally educated, she communicated in a spontaneous manner, much like a child. Her letters include images, metaphors and highly original interpretations of Christian doctrine. As mentioned, one of her most striking illustrative images in *The Dialogue* is that of the crucified Christ acting as a bridge between the divine and earthly spheres: three stages (the feet, the heart and the mouth) correspond to three movements of the soul (by afflictions, by love that mirrors the love of Christ and toward peace after its conflicts with sin). Karen Scott of DePaul University, an expert on Catherine's writings, said her letters are "characterized by a combination of didactic content, personal tone, and passionate concern to affect public matters and people's lives." Catherine, of course, believed her own writing was imbued with divine authority.

The language she used was emotionally charged, often filled with graphic references to food and Christ's flesh. For example, Catherine sometimes referred to conversion as the "eating of souls." The following provides another perfect example of the vivid language—phrases such as "mad with love"—that Catherine is known for:

O fire of love!
Was it not enough to gift us
with creation in your image and likeness,
and to create us anew to grace in your Son's blood,
without giving us yourself as food,
the whole of divine being,
the whole of God?
What drove you?
Nothing but your charity,
Mad with love as you are!

While Catherine was engaged in her many months of intense prayer in Rome, the dueling popes' all-too-public feud grew increasingly heated in 1378 and 1379. The spiritual anxiety that resulted crippled not only the Catholic Church as an institution but also the adherents to its teachings. The escalation of what was once a troublesome church problem into a full-blown diplomatic crisis was so swift that it left even the most devout Catholics suddenly doubting their faith. Both sides had dug themselves into intransigent positions, with neither pope willing to budge. Declaring a crusade against each other, both Urban and Clement asserted their right to create and confirm abbots, bishops and cardinals, so that there were eventually two Colleges of Cardinals and, in many places, two people claiming to hold the same elevated positions in the church. If a cardinal defected from one pope to another, the pope he left behind would simply appoint a new cardinal to replace him.

By the spring of 1379, the conflict within the church had become so intractable that both Urban and Clement had recruited and armed their own military forces with an eye toward settling the dispute—if necessary—by doing battle. And soon it came to just that. Clement organized a formidable band of Breton mercenaries to go after Urban. The army got off to an impressive start when they audaciously marched unchallenged into Roman territories and set up camp at Marino, about 15 miles south of Rome. They were absolutely perfect when it came to tactics and timing, seizing Castel Sant'Angelo, which until then had been an unassailable fortress, with little resistance. First built as a mausoleum in AD 129, the massive structure was turned into a military compound in 271. Due to its strategic location near the main entrance to St. Peter's, the takeover by Clement's men effectively kept Urban from using his own basilica. At the same time, Clement's ships patrolling the mouth of the Tiber prevented any reinforcements from getting to Urban down the river. All this left Urban backed into something of a corner, forced to take shelter at the Santa Maria church in Trastevere about a mile from the Vatican.

But Urban enjoyed at least some advantages. With the War of the Eight Saints over, Urban had the support of all the northern Italian city-states, including Florence, Siena and Milan, and he had the support of the Roman people. Both England and Poland backed him as well, promising monetary and military aid. Of course the French king, Charles V, supported Clement as he wanted nothing more than to reinstate the papacy in Avignon and to have a French pope—as did Giovanna of Naples. But more than all that, perhaps Urban's biggest advantage was Alberico di

Barbiano, the finest captain of the day. He had agreed to lead Urban's forces, made up exclusively of Italians. Barbiano had honed his battle skills with the help of none other than Sir John Hawkwood, and he had participated in the massacre of citizens at Cesena by Robert of Geneva—now Pope Clement. Once Barbiano came on board, word got out that Hawkwood, who was in the vicinity, might join Urban's band of mercenaries. Although the rumor proved false, it had scared Clement's men so much that more than a few abruptly defected, which allowed Urban's forces to make serious inroads.

Indeed, despite Clement's initial gains, Urban's troops went on to deliver a resounding blow to their opponents by orchestrating a brilliant two-pronged attack both in Rome and at Marino at the end of April 1379. First, Roman troops, supported by the Roman people, who were resentful of foreign domination, surrounded and assaulted the Castel Sant'Angelo. It wasn't long before the Bretons inside the fortress ran out of food, leaving them desperate. Everyone was just waiting for troops loyal to Clement to force their way into the city and come to their rescue, but as the weeks dragged on, that never happened. Finally, on April 27, the Bretons laid down their arms and the once-mighty French forces that had easily taken over Castel Sant'Angelo surrendered to Urban. Soon, Clement's beleaguered army also surrendered in Marino. Urban and his supporters couldn't have been more pleased as this was the first major engagement of the fourteenth century in which Italians defeated foreign mercenaries.

In the wake of these military setbacks, Clement and his cardinals had little choice but to vacate their position at Fondi, the city in central Italy where they had been staying, in search of someplace safe. Their best option, Clement concluded, was Giovanna's well-guarded court. And so in May 1379, the papal entourage traveled to Naples, where Giovanna—their biggest benefactor—gave them a magnificent reception. Not only did she grant Clement protection, but she also made a lavish public display of kissing his feet. But her people were not pleased by this deferential display.

The Neapolitan people favored their countryman, Urban, no matter how unstable he was or controversial his election. They therefore viewed Clement's presence in Naples with disdain and were particularly displeased by the homage paid by their queen to this outsider. When it appeared as though Clement and his cardinals intended to remain, the people took their fury to the streets, shouting "Long live Pope Urban!" as they looted French properties in the city. With an all-out rebellion unfolding, Clement realized he'd be risking his life if he stayed. Thanking Giovanna for her support, Clement and his cardinals quickly made a hasty escape to Gaeta, about 50 miles from Naples, and then set sail for Avignon, the city Gregory had left nearly three years earlier. There the party was greeted reverently by the six cardinals who had never left. Within weeks Clement and his men were happily resettled amid the luxurious trappings for which they had pined while in Italy.

Back in Rome, the people had been celebrating the Frenchmen's surrender. Basking in the adoration, Urban decided to make a show of walking barefoot as part of a dramatic procession from Santa Maria in Trastevere to St. Peter's, which was finally going to become the pope's home. Once there, Urban publicly thanked God for the double military victory, and the huge crowd of clergy and laity that surrounded him applauded his theatrical act of penance. While her correspondence does not expressly mention her participation, it is likely that Catherine joined in the procession and celebration. A few accounts—including Raymond's—report that she was the one who suggested Urban lead a procession and finally take up residence beside the grave of St. Peter.

A short time after the procession, on May 30, Catherine told Urban how pleased she was with the way the scene had played out. "I have been filled with joy at beholding with my eyes that holy procession, the likes of which has not been performed since the most remote ages. I rejoice that our sweet Mother Mary and St. Peter, the Prince of the Apostles, have restored you to your rightful residence," she wrote. "May the Eternal Truth grant you to make in your garden a garden of the servants of God, who may have nothing else to do than to pray for the prosperity of the Church and of your Holiness; for these are the soldiers who will obtain for you a complete victory."

With Clement having fled to Avignon, Catherine felt a renewed sense of purpose. Believing Urban's victory to be the perfect impetus for a revitalized pursuit of reconciliation, she used the opportunity to send out a flurry of new letters to those on both sides of the schism. In one, she wrote to King Charles, outlining all her arguments for the validity of Urban's election. She vilified the schismatics with the most scathing words she could think of. "Face up to the fact that you will surely die, and you don't know when. Set your sights on God and his truth, and not on emotion or love for your country. For where God is concerned we must be impartial, since all of us have come forth from his holy mind," she wrote. She ended by reminding the king that he had the "source of wisdom"—the University of Paris—at his fingertips. The university had at first recognized Urban as pope, but in May 1379 it had caved in to pressure from the king and sided with Clement.

In another letter, Catherine warned Giovanna that she could die unless she returned to the true faith. "Oh, do not wait for the time when perhaps no time will be granted you! Do not force my eyes to stream with tears for your wretched body and soul!" For some reason, Catherine always felt a certain kinship with Giovanna, who had been married four times, and she wrote at least seven long letters to the blond-haired ruler. Although her court was often criticized for its excessive frills—including a vast collection of exotic animals—the queen professed to be deeply spiritual. But despite her affection for the queen, Catherine was never blind to her shortcomings.

And Catherine was about to be even more disappointed with her. Even with Clement back in Avignon, civil unrest, stoked by the population's overall displeasure with Giovanna, had continued to spread in Naples. Giovanna knew she had to do something to win back her people's loyalty—something dramatic. And so she publicly announced a sudden switch in allegiances. She sent her representatives to Rome, ostensibly to make peace with Urban. Catherine was thrilled, believing that the queen was having a true change of heart. But that happiness was short-lived, as it was all a ploy. Giovanna had said she was supporting Urban only as a way to bide some time while her husband amassed a German force large enough to put down the insurrection. She recalled her representatives from Rome and once again threw her support behind Clement. The whole thing had been a pretense. There was no way she'd support Urban: just after his election as pope in 1378, Urban had tried to take Naples away from her and cede part of her kingdom to his nephew Francesco Prigano. Giovanna would never forgive him for it.

Again, Catherine begged Giovanna to come to her senses: "I long for your salvation with all my soul, but . . . if you do not renounce this error and other sins . . . Neither your riches, nor your power, nor your worldly honors, nor the barons or people who are your temporal subjects can protect you from the wrath of Almighty God, and shield you from Divine Justice."

It's not clear what Catherine knew of this, but Urban had been making his own plans to get back at Giovanna, putting in motion a plot to overthrow the queen. For assistance, the pope had reached out to Charles of Durazzo, a cousin of King Louis I of Hungary and second cousin of Giovanna, to suggest that Charles march on Naples and claim the kingdom for himself, with the backing of Louis's army. Urban told Charles he would clear the way for the intervention by declaring the queen deposed and sanctioning an invasion of the kingdom. Charles, of course, was flattered and considered the idea—but ultimately declined the offer.

Urban, too, got distracted by other endeavors, with his greatest challenge at the time being a lack of money. Not only had he spent dearly on the hiring of Italian mercenaries, but he also could no longer rely on the income he had previously received from Giovanna and the others who had taken Clement's side. Their money, of course, was now going to prop up Clement in Avignon. As if that weren't bad enough, payments to the pope by the Italian city-states mandated by the treaty ending the War of Eight Saints were in arrears. Not knowing where else to turn, Urban put Catherine to work as something of a debt collector.

It was a role she already had been filling, as is intimated by a letter she had sent to the Florentine leaders earlier that year reminding them to pay up: "You have been put back at the breast of the holy Church, and can receive the fruits of the blood. If only you want it, from Pope Urban VI, true pontiff and Christ's vicar on earth. And now you see him in such great need, and not only are you not helping him, but you are paying no attention to what you had promised. So you are showing yourselves very ungrateful." She sent a similar letter to the leaders of Perugia: "I long to see you coming to the aid of your father. You would be helping yourselves as well, since by helping him you are helping along your own spiritual and temporal welfare. You are . . . coming to the aid of this dear bride, holy Church, and Pope Urban VI, you are paying what you owe—and by paying it we show our gratitude and appreciation to God, as well as to the pope for all the favors he has continually done for us."

Catherine wrote many other letters related to the schism during this time—perhaps as many as 60—including one to the Augustinian hermit William Flete. Urban had asked him, as he had asked Catherine, to come to Rome as a special adviser during the schism. But Flete, as usual, refused to leave the peace and tranquility of the Augustinian monastery of Lecceto where he resided. During the fourteenth century, Lecceto had become the base of the Augustinians' observant movement, which advocated a return to the primitive character of the Augustinians as hermits. Surrounded by land dotted with caves and the most beautiful oak trees, Lecceto was paradise for a reflective man such as Flete. Like other hermits, he desired a greater spiritual intensity through solitude and contemplation and spent his days praying in a cave and his nights sleeping at the monastery. His love of solitude was so great that even the pope's cry for help didn't cause him to give it up. An exasperated Catherine—who had visited many times at Lecceto and so understood the location's appeal—argued in her letter that God is to be found everywhere and that one shouldn't be so attached to a single place.

"Today we see the Church in such need that to help it we must deny ourselves by coming out of our woods. Seeing that you can bear fruit in the Church, this is not the time for you to stand still or to say, 'I won't have any peace,'" she told him. "Now that God has given us the grace of providing holy Church with a good, just shepherd whose delight is God's servants whom he wishes to have near him, and who hopes to be able to purify the Church by uprooting vice and planting virtue without fear, we others ought to support him in his just and courageous behavior."

Catherine had no patience for anyone who lacked the courage to get the job done—and that was even more true for those closest to her. When Raymond had tried to enter France in order to press Urban's case with King Charles, he was warned that soldiers were waiting to ambush him. If he kept going, he would almost certainly be taken prisoner, possibly even killed. Raymond decided to turn back to Genoa. Catherine was displeased, believing the move to be cowardly. She wrote him: "I long to see you raised this very day above your childishness, a courageous man. Grow beyond liking milk, and become a bread eater, because children who feed on milk are incapable of going into battle; they only enjoy playing games with those of their age. You weren't worthy to stand for even a little while on the battlefield. No, like a child, you were driven off—and you willingly fled, very happy that God had made concessions to your weakness."

In the summer of 1379, Raymond disappointed her again by failing to be a martyr a second time. After rerouting the journey through Spain, Urban had sent Raymond back to France to visit Charles. But because Spain had opted to go over to Clement's side, the road through Spain was effectively shut off, which thwarted Raymond's plans yet again. Raymond wrote about his unsuccessful attempt to reach France to Catherine, asking her not to use her high standards to judge his lack of progress: "[You don't] think I should measure you by my standards." She fired back:

So you were suspecting that my love and affection for you had lessened. But you didn't realize—though you showed it to be true—that your love had diminished while mine had grown. For I love you with the same love with which I love myself, and I firmly believe that God in his goodness will provide what is lacking on your part. But it didn't work out that way, for you've found ways of throwing off the load. You ought to be dead but aren't. So make an effort to kill yourself with the knife of hatred and love so that you won't hear the mockery and vilification and reproach the world and the persecutors of holy Church may choose to give you . . . I tell you, dearest father, whether we want it or not, these times invite us to die—so for my sake, stop being alive! Let's gladly give our bodies to the wild beasts.

Within her family of followers, Catherine had been crystal clear about her position: all of them needed to be what God wanted them to be and if that meant dying for their faith, then so be it. That was especially true when it came to Raymond. She berated Raymond for his timidity, an older man who was her own spiritual adviser, the one who was supposed to be directing her. At some point in the latter half of 1379, Catherine and her family of followers relocated from their home on Via del Corso in Rome into a somewhat larger house near the Santa Maria sopra Minerva— their preferred place of worship—on the street that is now called Via di Santa Chiara. Whether in Rome or elsewhere, Catherine and her women followers slept in shared living quarters—the men shared another nearby space—and they all came together daily for meals and to attend Mass. Catherine was not only the mother figure who tended to everyone's needs, she was also the very heart and soul of the group. At the end of a long day, they often gathered on the floor at her feet to pray with her, just as the disciples had done with Jesus. Because begging was frowned upon (the fourteenth century is when many European cities enacted anti-begging legislation), Catherine and her followers relied on the kindness of those who admired her teachings for food and shelter. In return, they divvied up domestic duties.

One story circulated by early biographers involved an occasion in 1379 in Rome when someone—perhaps it was Catherine, but we don't know for sure—forgot to pick up bread for the house. This upset the others, as pilgrims from Siena were joining them for supper and there wasn't nearly enough food to go around. Catherine told them not to worry and asked the servers to go ahead and distribute whatever bread they had on hand. As in the Gospel story of the loaves and fishes, bread kept materializing and they wound up with more at the end of the meal than they had had at the beginning. Miracles involving food were often attributed to Catherine—someone who did not eat.

From her new residence in Rome, Catherine wrote to one of her favorite secretaries, Neri di Landoccio, of how she missed her hometown of Siena, especially at Easter. Quite possibly she sensed that she would never see her beloved city again. "In your nature, Eternal Divinity, I have learned to know my own nature," she said in one of the last prayers. "My nature is fire."

But by this time that fire was nearly extinguished. The weight of her own inadequacies in the face of so many challenges—the schism, the failure to reform the church, the bizarre behavior of the pope, the fickleness of the Romans—bore down on her. According to Raymond, her distress over the Romans was actually starting to play tricks on her mind. He cited one vision in which "she saw in spirit the whole city of Rome filled with demons busy in every quarter inciting the populace to the murder of their father. As she continued praying they turned on her with dreadful shouts, crying, 'Curse you, it is you who are trying to stop us; but no! we have marked you out for a fearful death, and there is no escape for you.'" Besides being consumed with worry, Catherine still wasn't eating. And she barely slept more than 30 minutes at a time. Proof of a deterioration in her condition is the dramatic reduction in the number of letters dictated between the summer and fall of 1379.

What little energy she did have she expended trekking back and forth each day through the crowded streets of Rome to St. Peter's—which had become her favorite place to pray. Anyone of a pious nature would have been drawn to St. Peter's, the old basilica that stood on the spot where the new St. Peter's Basilica stands today in Vatican City. It was an incredible space, capable of holding up to 4,000 worshippers at a time. Inside were five aisles, a wide central nave and two smaller aisles off to each side, which were divided by 21 marble columns on each side. Over 350 feet long, it was built in the shape of a cross, illuminated by light filtered through clerestory windows in the upper walls. Everywhere there were beautiful frescoes depicting people and scenes from both the Old and the New Testaments. But the edifice—built in the fourth century—had cracks in its structure, and Catherine wished it could be rebuilt. Urban had promised her that he'd start the process, but he never followed through. By the fifteenth century, the church had fallen into complete ruin. Soon the weaknesses in the building's walls and beams had become so extreme that the church had to be demolished to make way for the construction of a new building.

If Catherine hadn't looked healthy before, January 1380 brought an even more startling decline in her physical condition. According to Barduccio di Piero Canigiani, the Florentine notary who became one of her closest followers during the last few years of her life, she was taking no nourishment at all. "The food necessary for her bodily sustenance excited in her such horror that it was impossible for her to swallow it. She could not, for her refreshment, even drink a single drop of water, though she was consumed with burning thirst, and her throat was so parched that she seemed to breathe fire," he wrote. Yet somehow she continued to muster enough energy to pray with her family members, dictate a few more letters and make her way each day to St. Peter's.

But then, at the end of the month, there was a most peculiar change in her condition that worried everyone who loved her.

TWELVE

The End of a Saintly Existence

On Sunday, January 29, 1380, Catherine suffered a stroke while visiting St. Peter's, one so virulent it seemed as though it had killed her. That's how it appeared to Barduccio di Piero Canigiani, one of her disciples. He reported that Catherine had "so violent a stroke that from that day onwards she was no longer in health."

But just as he and others were preparing themselves for her imminent passing, she suddenly sprang back to life after hours of lying prostrate on the floor. The color returned to her cheeks and she once again displayed the resilience that always distinguished her from everybody else. And yet, Barduccio said, Catherine "did not seem the same person as she who had fallen." As the days went on, something was very different. Her physical suffering intensified, but so did her devotion to prayer. As Barduccio wrote to his sister in early February: "I think you know that her prayers were of such intensity that one hour of prayer more consumed that poor little body than two days upon the rack would have done another. Therefore every morning with tears we lifted her up after Communion in such a state that those who so saw her deemed her dead and carried her to her couch. And after an hour or two she would rise up, and we went to San Pietro, and then she set herself to prayer, and she remained there till nearly vespers, after which she returned home so exhausted that she seemed a dead woman, and thus she continued every day."

From Catherine's point of view, the breakdown she had suffered that day was "mystical" in nature, not related to her physical health. In one of her last letters to Raymond, dated February 15, 1380, she described the spiritual experience she had withstood—joyfully—during which she was privy to all the many mysteries of God and his kingdom. "Father! Father and sweetest son! Stupendous mysteries has God accomplished since the Feast of the Circumcision [January 1], such that the tongue alone cannot tell of them. But passing over all that period, let us come to Sexagesima Sunday [January 29] for it was then those mysteries occurred that you will hear of in the brief account I am giving you, quite unlike anything I have ever experienced. So intense was the pain in my heart that my tunic was torn through my clutching at as much of it as I could while I writhed in the chapel like one convulsed. Had anyone tried to hold me, he would surely have robbed me of life," she wrote.

While on the floor, Catherine had a vision in which she asked God, "What can I do, oh immense Fire?" God answered that she should "offer your life once more, and never let yourself rest. This was the task I set you, and now set you again, you and all who follow you." God continued with what seemed to be an endorsement of Urban, saying, "See his good holy intention . . . And just as the bride is alone, so is he alone. I am allowing him to use immoderately the means he uses, as well as the fear he inspires in his subjects, to sweep holy Church clean."

As the vision went on, Catherine said, "God set me in his presence. True, I'm always present to him because he holds all within himself, but this was in a new way, as if my memory and understanding and will had nothing to do with my body. And I was gazing into this Truth with such light that at that point everything became fresh—the mysteries of holy Church and all the graces I've received during my life, past and present."

God told the holy woman—the conscience of a church in crisis—to instruct Urban to forge unity, as she had done so many times before, and to urge the cardinals to adopt a more conciliatory nature.

She told Raymond that she better understood now how "no one can come to enjoy God's beauty within the depths of the Trinity except through this dear bride (the church)—since we must all pass through the gate of Christ crucified, and this gate is found only in holy Church." Again, this was verification that—in Catherine's eyes—the only way to God was through the church, no matter how unappetizing the pope.

She also wrote to tell Raymond, her adviser, how he could be more holy. "I don't want you to look back because of any persecution, but glory in adversity. It is by enduring that we manifest our love and constancy, and render glory to God's name. Now is the time, dear father, to lose yourself completely and to think nothing about yourself . . . ," she said.

The following day, Catherine dictated a final political missive to Urban in which she exhorted him in very clear language to govern the church with prudence, especially in his dealings with the Romans, many of whom still supported Clement. Although Rome was believed to be the true seat of the papacy, there were even some Italians who acknowledged that Avignon was an effective location where leadership could be centralized. "Receive them with all the sweetness that you can, pointing out to them what is necessary, as you see fit. Pardon me—for love makes me say what perhaps doesn't need to be said—but you must know the nature of your Roman children, of how they are led and bound more by gentleness than by any other force or by harsh words," she wrote. "And you know, too, the great necessity that there is for you and holy Church to preserve these people in obedience and reverence—because in that is the beginning of faith." She also urged Urban to steer away from the impulsive behavior he had become known for: "I want to see you governing holy Church and your little sheep so wisely that it will never be necessary to reverse anything your holiness has done or ordained, not even the least word, so that both God and human beings may always see a firmness grounded in truth."

She reminded him that he needed the Romans and that they needed him. Then she added, "And forgive me, dearest and most holy father, for saying these things to you. I trust that your humility and kindness welcome such words, and that you do not scorn and distain them because they come from the mouth of a very contemptible woman. For the humble consider not who is speaking but only God's honor, the truth, and their own salvation."

She had barely finished dictating the letter when another round of intense physical pain made her double over in what was perhaps the continuation of the "stroke"—to use Barduccio's word—she'd had the previous day. Her body went limp but exhibited no apparent outward signs of sickness. Just as when she received the stigmata in 1375, there was real physical agony but no conspicuous symptoms. She felt as though she were surrounded by devils, she told Raymond, tormenting her while unclean spirits gripped her body. Even when she was unconscious, she was very aware of the assaults. She described them to Raymond as "the most terrible I have ever endured. I simply do not know what the divine Goodness will choose to do with me but, judging how my body feels, it seems to me that I must seal all this period with a fresh martyrdom in my soul's beloved, that is, in holy church."

On one level she must have realized that all this suffering might have been a side effect of her poor diet, chronic stress and lack of sleep. But on another level the demons raining down on her seemed very real, and she fought them off with all her might by repeating: "God come to my help, O Lord hasten and come to my help." This physical storm raged for two days and two nights, after which she finally seemed well enough to attend Mass. February 2 was the Feast of the Purification of Mary, a day of renewal celebrated 40 days after Christmas. Catherine felt reinvigorated by the service, which honored the obedience of one of her great role models, the Virgin Mary.

Because she never knew when another attack might come on, Catherine didn't waste any time during the next few weeks. Every spare minute she had, she passed along words of wisdom to those who had meant so much to her. One of the papal secretaries, Tommaso Petra, visited Catherine during this time, urging her to prescribe a specific course of action for each of her disciples so that they might know what to do after she was gone. "Leave us," he begged, "all rich in divine love by this last will and testament, for I am certain that this injunction will be most pleasing to the Lord."

She told Raymond to remain faithful to the "little ship, holy Church." She asked him to take care of her book while also acting as a shepherd, governor and father to their family. She asked Alessia Saracini to take over the care and guidance of the Mantellate. She decided that Stefano Maconi should join the Carthusian order and that Neri di Landoccio should become a hermit. She had mapped out precise plans for each and every one of them.

She instructed them to love and care for one another. "By this shall all men know that you are my disciples, if you have love one for another," she said. "And I promise you that I shall be with you always, and be of much more use to you on the other side than I ever could be here on earth, for then I shall have left the darkness behind me and move in the eternal light." She told them to be zealous in prayer, both vocal (at fixed hours) and mental (continuously). In addition, she said they should never judge their neighbors or gossip about what they might be doing. "We must never judge the will of a creature," she said. "Even if we see a thing to be a manifest sin, we must not pass judgment on it."

As often as she could, she still made her way to St. Peter's, supporting herself by leaning on the shoulders of her disciples, to pray for the church and for her followers—the two causes closest to her heart. When she felt well enough, she spent one to two hours praying in the morning in her room and then a few hours more praying in the afternoon at St. Peter's. She fretted constantly over what might become of her followers when she was no longer around.

Always when she left the basilica at the end of the day she was confronted with the large and famous mosaic the Florentine artist Giotto di Bondone had created for the atrium in honor of the Jubilee year of 1300. This icon of faith depicted the story from the Gospel of Matthew of Christ walking on water in the Sea of Tiberias. Christ summons Peter to do the same while the apprehensive apostles look on from their storm-ravaged boat. Peter allows fear to overwhelm him, though, and he starts to drown, causing Christ to shout out, "Courage! It's me! Don't be afraid. You have so little faith. Why did you doubt?" Popularly known as

Navicella, or "Little Ship," the mosaic spoke to Catherine, as it did to every worshipper leaving the church. Giotto's sense of perspective wasn't perfect, and it almost looked as though the boat shown in the background was being propped up by Peter's back. Just as Christ did not let Peter sink, the Catholic Church expected the papacy to survive all challenges with the help of the Lord.

Leaving the basilica one Sunday in late February, Catherine's eyes naturally gravitated to Giotto's mosaic, as they always did, but this time it seemed as though the entire boat—or the whole of the church—was pressing down on her own back, not on Peter's. The weight of it was too much for her frail body, and she slumped to the ground like a rag doll. Alarmed, her companions rushed to help her, but even when she regained consciousness, her legs were too weak to hold her up. Together, they carried her back to her home, but now she was completely immobilized by physical pain. Barduccio declared that for eight weeks she was "both internally and externally tormented . . . unable to lift her head." The lack of food and water over so many months didn't help, having whittled her body to nothing but skin and bones. According to Barduccio, "She often said, 'These are not bodily or natural pains, but it seems that I have given permission to the demons to torment this body at their will.' It seemed to be thus, for Catherine endured the most grievous pains ever heard, and it would seem to be profane to tell you of her patience. This much I tell you: When a new agony came, she raised her eyes with joy to God and said, 'Thanks be to you, eternal bridegroom, who grants gifts and graces to me, a wretched woman and unworthy servant, every day.'"

Her close friend and follower Bartolomeo Dominici, who was now prior of a monastery in Siena, returned to Rome in time for Easter, which fell on March 25 that year. The day was also Catherine's thirty-third birthday. When he saw her, he was stunned. He barely recognized the shriveled-up woman on the bed before him. He didn't dare leave her in such a state and celebrated Easter Mass for her and her followers in her room as bells sounded from all of Rome's churches. To everyone's astonishment Catherine somehow managed to get up and out of bed and receive Communion, the only sustenance she'd had for months. Afterward, he told her that, given her condition, he felt terrible leaving Rome, but that he felt obligated to do so. She encouraged him to go, saying, "Son, you know what a consolation it is for me to have near me the children whom God has given me. I should be so happy if Raymond could be here too. But it is God's will that I am to be without you both." The following morning, he came by to say farewell and reported her looking "merry and bright." She found the strength to lift her arms and wrap them around his neck in a final embrace. He would never see her again.

For another month, Catherine clung to life, all while enduring what Barduccio called "terrible and unheard-of agony." During those moments when she felt the most severe pain, she always stopped for a moment to thank God for giving her the ability to suffer so greatly. Tommaso Caffarini had this to say of her last days: "She bore everything with such a steady courage and cheerfulness that it was as though it was not she herself who suffered these terrible pains. She always spoke so calmly and lovingly that all who heard her were full of admiration. She always spoke of God's glory, of gratitude for the salvation of men, and of the eternal happiness of her neighbor. And although she suffered physically more than words can tell, the expression on her face was always as happy and good as an angel's."

Finally, on the morning of April 29, she underwent what Barduccio called another "great change." Catherine's face had become as puckered as a very old woman's, with dark circles under her eyes.

Her body looked shorter, shrunken. In bed, she could just barely move her head and arms, while her legs seemed paralyzed. Everyone was summoned—her mother Lapa, Alessia and her other female friends, Neri di Landoccio and her many other secretaries. Giovanni Tantucci, described as a Master of Sacred Theology, gave her the absolution, or *a culpa et a poena*, an indulgence granted by the pope at the hour of death. This popular phrase during the late Middle Ages means that the sinner is freed from both the penalty *(poena)* of sins against God and neighbor, and also from the guilt *(culpa)* of those sins.

As Barduccio described it, Catherine made a long, rambling speech with shards of lucidity but no coherent narrative. Again and again, she said, "I have sinned against God, have mercy." And once, after having been silent for a while, she said with a jubilant countenance, as if in response to someone or something asking her a question: "Never vainglory, but always the true glory and praise of Jesus Christ crucified." At one point, those present described her darkened face, shaking rapidly from side to side, though her eyes stayed closed. She cried out, "God come to my help. The true glory of Christ crucified." And with that, her dying face turned radiantly happy. Her eyes opened and brightened, and it looked as though she had won a final battle against the demons. She smiled and said, "Praised be our beloved Savior."

As Alessia held her head on her breast, Catherine fixed her eyes on the crucifix. She humbly asked Lapa for her blessing. Lapa sat weeping at her daughter's side. She tried to find some consolation when she asked Catherine to bless her in return and prayed that she should not sin against God's will by being sad for too long.

Catherine continued to pray right until the last moment, for Urban, for her family, for her church. Her face was as beautiful as an angel's, and she seemed at peace.

According to Barduccio, she spoke like someone who never stopped craving the blood of Christ. "Lord, you summon me to yourself, and I am coming, not by my own merits, but solely through your mercy, which I crave from you in virtue of your blood." After all that, she shouted out over and over: *"Sangue, Sangue!"* (Italian for "blood"), startling everyone around her. Finally, imitating the example of Christ on the cross, she said, "Father, into your hands I commend my soul and my spirit." At about 12:00 p.m., Catherine made the sign of the cross and died. One witness wrote that she died "sweetly, with a face all shining and angelical, she bent her head, and gave up the ghost."

On the day of her death, Raymond was in his monastery at Genoa preparing for his journey to Bologna. He was meant to first travel by sea to Pisa, but the weather had deteriorated. He went up the stairs to the dormitories, stopping before a picture of Catherine in the hallway. A clear voice materialized out of thin air that spoke directly to his soul, telling him: "Do not be afraid, I am here for your sake, I am in heaven for your sake." Greatly bewildered, he wondered who was giving him these promises of security. Later, while in Bologna, where he was elected Master General of the Dominicans, he heard that Catherine had died at precisely the same moment that he heard the mysterious voice that had so reassured and encouraged him.

Catherine's disciples tried to keep her death a secret, fearing a mob scene, but word spread quickly in a place like Rome, where any unusual activity or movement aroused suspicion. Her devoted secretary Stefano carried her body to the Santa Maria sopra Minerva church. Within no time, throngs of people began arriving, longing to catch a glimpse of her, to kiss her feet and hands, to touch her one final time, or perhaps to snatch a snippet of her clothing or something else as a keepsake of the saintly woman. So large was the horde that soon the coffin had to be moved behind the iron railings in the chapel. But still they came.

Her body was left unburied for two or three days and, as some accounts tell it, it was "without any odor being perceptible, her body remaining so pure, intact, and fragrant, that her arms, her neck and her legs remained as flexible as if she were still alive."

The endless parade of people at the eventual funeral created such a commotion that when Giovanni Tantucci went up to the pulpit to deliver the eulogy, he was unable to make himself heard above the tumult. He mumbled, "This holy virgin has no need of our preaching. She preached sufficiently herself," as he climbed down.

Raymond described in detail eight miraculous cures attributed to Catherine that had occurred in the days immediately after her death, before she was buried. There might have been others, he acknowledged, but he wrote that he wanted to relay only those instances where he had seen the miracles for himself or had the opportunity to examine the people who had been healed. In one case, while her body was still in the church, a nun who had not been able to use one of her arms for six months due to an infirmity went to the church but was not able to get near the body because of the crowds. She gave her veil to somebody else and asked that person to touch Catherine's body with it. According to Raymond, when she got the veil back and put it next to her arm, she was immediately cured.

In another case, a four-year-old boy who had not been able to keep his head straight without pain due to some problem with his neck was finally able to get close enough to touch Catherine's body. The boy at once began to heal and was able to straighten his head. A woman with leprosy placed the affected parts of her body near Catherine's hands and her condition improved instantly. Soon there was not even the slightest sign of leprosy on her skin.

In one of the more extraordinary accounts of miracles, Raymond wrote of a servant woman named Bona di Giovanni who, while washing a quilt, leaned over too far, fell into the river and was whisked away by a fast current. She cried out, "O holy virgin, Catherine of Siena, save me from this great danger!" Immediately, and in broad daylight, witnesses saw her levitate off the water and through the air, all the way back to the bank, with the quilt still in her hands. According to various accounts, Catherine herself had also been seen levitating while praying at certain points in her life.

Raymond said that the miracles didn't stop even after Catherine was buried. A boy named Giacomo had been in bed for many months with a serious illness and seemed to be near death. After all hope of saving him was gone, a particularly pious woman consecrated him to Catherine and at once the boy regained his strength. In another instance, a man named Giovanni di Tozzo with a terrible eye issue went to visit Catherine's grave and was completely healed. In still another case, a small boy who could not walk was brought to her tomb, and, as soon as he was held over it, his feet and legs grew strong and he could move about as if nothing had ever been wrong with him.

Of course, Raymond was Catherine's most loyal defender, and his account of her life, in which he recounts these miracles and more, was designed to make a case for sainthood. Like her other early biographers, Raymond most likely tried to play up her role as a contemplative mystic with a faith so profound she was able to perform miracles. Although Catherine's greatest strength was in her highly personal and mystical relationship with God, no person can be made a saint without having miracles attributed to him or her unless, of course, they were martyred for their faith. The number of miracles in causes of canonization has varied over the centuries, and historians aren't sure if two or three miracles—supposedly performed after death—were officially attributed to Catherine for canonization. It's also possible that a papal dispensation was granted. Unfortunately, the record isn't clear.

Catherine was first buried in the cemetery of Santa Maria sopra Minerva, which lies virtually next to the Pantheon. Sometime later Raymond moved her grave inside the church, where it would not be exposed to the weather. It is believed that her head and thumb were severed from her body during this move and were transported to Siena in the spring of 1383. Apparently the people of her hometown demanded to have at least a part of her. A story is often told of how the Sienese—knowing that they would never get away with smuggling Catherine's entire body out of Rome—decided to take only her head and thumb, which they placed in a bag. When stopped by Roman guards, they prayed for Catherine's help. When they opened the bag to show the guards, there were only rose petals inside. Once they got back to Siena, they reopened the bag, and her head and thumb were there as before. Thanks to this story, Catherine is often portrayed holding a rose. One can only imagine how triumphant Lapa must have felt to know that at least a part of her daughter had come back to her birthplace. Later, Catherine's body was moved again to the Chapel of the Rosary and finally laid to rest under the high altar in Santa Maria sopra Minerva, where it now lies.

Exhuming bodies after burial isn't all that unusual in the history of the Catholic Church. For example, the body of another famous Catherine, St. Catherine of Bologna, sits to this day eerily upright on a golden throne behind a glass case inside the Church of the Saint in Bologna.

When it comes to Catherine of Siena, her mummified head sits today in an ornate reliquary in the San Domenico Basilica in Siena. Dramatically lit, the somewhat macabre skull—wrapped in a white nun's habit—has weathered the centuries well. Perched on a beautiful marble altar built by Giovanni di Stefano, her shriveled face, minus the nose, seems to stare out from behind the glass at the steady stream of people who visit the site every day. Her lone digit, on display in a smaller reliquary near the head, seems to be giving the church an eternal thumbs-up.

After Catherine's death, Raymond worked on the book about her life for 15 years. When he finished, Lapa and Catherine's beloved sister-in-law, Lisa Colombini, were still alive, but Alessia Saracini and several other disciples from whom he received his information were already dead. Lapa, who outlived most of her children and many of her grandchildren, helped Raymond write his biography of her daughter and was feisty and outspoken until the end, complaining, "I think God has laid my soul athwart in my body, so it can't get out." Four years after finishing the book, Raymond died while in Nuremberg. He was nearly 70 years old. As Master General of the Dominicans, he had worked unremittingly until the end for strict adherence to the rules laid down by St. Dominic. He also had kept up Catherine's fight for a peaceful solution to the schism crisis. Raymond's body was later transferred to Naples. On the fifth centenary of his death, Raymond was beatified by Pope Leo XIII. For more than four years, he had been spiritual adviser to a saint whose career was unprecedented in history. By all accounts, he had carried out his duties faithfully.

In the years just after Catherine's death, the papacy spiraled further downward into despair, as all thoughts of reformation vacated the pope's heart. Without Catherine, there was no longer a check on Urban's vices, and his harsh measures—which included the murder of several cardinals suspected of disloyalty—disgraced his pontificate. With Clement in France, Urban set his sights on going after Naples, the only stronghold his French nemesis had in Italy. In April 1380, he went so far as to depose Giovanna in a vain attempt to make an unworthy Charles of Durazzo king after he promised to hand over part of his kingdom to Urban's nephew. Two years later, Giovanna died at the age of 54, reportedly murdered, possibly by Hungarian soldiers. Urban died in the Vatican on October 15, 1389, apparently from injuries suffered when he fell off his mule. Although he had set out as a seemingly vigorous reformer of the church and a friend of Catherine's, he ended his days still meddling in Neapolitan politics with almost no support. The schismatic church continued for another three decades after Urban's death as Catholics across Europe became increasingly disheartened. Catherine had worked as a tireless campaigner for church reform and was never afraid to say exactly what she was feeling. Sadly, her quixotic ambitions had not paid off.

EPILOGUE

A Woman's Legacy

In September 2015, Americans got their first up-close look at one of the most beloved religious figures in recent history, Pope Francis, during his visits to Philadelphia, New York City and Washington, D.C.

When Jorge Mario Bergoglio was elected pope—and took the name Francis—in March 2013, the Roman Catholic Church was at a pivotal moment in history, its political and moral influence waning in an increasingly secular modern-day world. The 266th pontiff inherited an institution beset by scandal, wrestling with a whole host of challenges that only had been exacerbated by the waning energy of his aging predecessor, Benedict XVI. These included a shortage of priests, an ongoing and rampant sexual abuse crisis, a perception the church had become out of touch and a flow of defectors to evangelical churches in the Southern Hemisphere.

With his humble, simple exterior, Pope Francis has captivated both Catholics and non-Catholics everywhere by eschewing the costumes, palaces and pageantry of previous popes and by making mercy the bedrock of his ministry. He's cold-called nuns, blasted the "unfettered pursuit of money" and refused to pass judgment on gay people—all while reaching out to atheists. A Pew Research Center survey conducted in February 2015 found that the nearly 80-year-old pontiff's favorability rating among U.S. Catholics had shot up to 90 percent, rivaling that of even Pope John Paul II in the 1980s and 1990s. The man dubbed "the people's pope" said he chose to be named after the mystic St. Francis of Assisi, "the man of poverty, the man of peace, the man who loves and protects creation," because he wished for a "poor Church, for the poor." Since taking the reins of the Catholic Church, Pope Francis has repeatedly railed against trickle-down economics, global warming and a "culture of waste" that values profit over people.

Although Pope Francis's popularity may not have resulted in a flood of new Catholic converts—not yet anyway—there's no denying that this plain-spoken Argentine, with his willingness to talk about doubt and his shunning of the Vatican's "pope suite" and other niceties, appeals to a wide array of people and has inspired many to take a closer look at the Catholic faith—including its saints.

I have a feeling that Catherine, a minister to the poor and plague-stricken, would have been mightily pleased. Like the pope, she cared not a whit for the trappings of wealth. But she did care about her beloved Italy and the Catholic Church. Unfortunately, in the decades after her death, the two were in a more lamentable state than when she had left them. The papacy was immeasurably more corrupt than it had been even during the time of the Avignon Papacy, with far more serious divisions about to erupt. Within a few short decades, there would be three—not two—claimants to the papacy. This occurred when, in an attempt to end the schism, cardinals on both sides of the divide convened a meeting in Pisa in 1409 to elect a new pope—Alexander V. But the two "existing" popes refused to step aside, resulting in a stalemate—and three popes. Even so, the true value of the work to which all the years of Catherine's life were dedicated—as well as those of her not insignificant band of disciples—cannot be measured only by their conspicuous and immediate effects on the religious institution she fought so hard to preserve. Her model of spirituality was mystical as well as political, and her way of diving into the thick of the social issues of her era has stood the test of time. The way she maintained and shared her joy, even amid profound suffering, speaks to people today.

On April 30, 2014, Pope Francis recalled the life of St. Catherine of Siena before a large audience of Catholics. Evoking her example, he encouraged the young to "learn from her how to live with the clear conscience of those who do not bend to human compromises." He told the sick to be inspired by "her example of strength in the moments of greatest pain," and newlyweds to "imitate the solidity of faith of those who trust in God."

A few years earlier, in 2010, Pope Benedict XVI also invoked Catherine's example, saying, "like the Sienese saint, every believer feels the need to be conformed with the sentiments of the heart of Christ to love God and his neighbor as Christ himself loves. Dear brothers and sisters, let us learn from St. Catherine to love Christ and the Church with courage in an intense and sincere way."

The stigmata, the mystical marriage and the miracles attributed to St. Catherine may seem inconceivable to skeptics. But so do so many other traditions related to the saints, especially as considered from our contemporary vantage point. The exhumation of bodies decades after their deaths, for instance, may leave even the believers of today incredulous. Visiting the Basilica of San Domenico in Siena and viewing Catherine's head and finger on display—while knowing that the rest of her body is in

Rome—may seem bizarre, to say the least. But Catholicism—which is anything but a squeamish religion—venerates the bodies and body parts of the faithful departed.

Rather than view Catherine through the prism of modernity, one must consider the way her life and teachings transgressed the boundaries placed upon women during her time. Yes, it was Catherine, along with Bridget of Sweden, who paved the way for the likes of Joan of Arc, the more widely known symbol of French unity who was officially canonized in 1920, as well as for other female religious rock stars of the fifteenth and sixteenth centuries.

Although famous during her own lifetime, in the years immediately after her death, Catherine achieved something of a cult status thanks in large part to her most devoted and tireless friend, Raymond of Capua. Raymond laid the groundwork for all later considerations of Catherine by publishing the first and most authoritative story of her life. *The Life of St. Catherine of Siena* was written in Latin and completed in 1395, four years before Raymond's death. Translated into many languages, it soon spread word of Catherine and her godliness across Christian Europe, and eventually around the world. The book also put Raymond on the map. It appeared in an English translation during the fifteenth century as the *Lyf of St. Katherin of Senis* and has been retranslated and republished many times since. The book was not a biography in the modern sense, being more of a biased plea for sainthood than a traditional chronology of her life, yet it represented a real advancement in the art of hagiography. Unlike other writers, Raymond actually took the time and care to interview people who had known Catherine, including her mother, Lapa. Raymond's book tells only of what he experienced firsthand—or heard about firsthand. It also highlights the many accounts of miracles attributed to Catherine's intercession—including those that occurred after her death, since posthumous miracles are essential for canonization. Even so, Tommaso Caffarini may have felt Raymond characterized Catherine's life with some restrictions because after the book appeared, Caffarini put together a collection of stories around 1414—based on his own personal experiences—called *Libellus de Supplemento Legende Prolixe Virginis Beate Catherine de Senis*, which included some stories that Raymond apparently had overlooked. Today we are fortunate to have the benefit of more readable translations of Catherine's own landmark work, *The Dialogue*, in addition to Raymond's and Tommaso's biographies.

After Raymond's death, Caffarini championed the case for Catherine's sainthood from Venice. Before dying in 1434—the last person in Catherine's inner circle to pass away—Caffarini had succeeded in organizing the notes and writings of Catherine's first confessor, Tommaso della Fonte. When people complained about the Dominicans publicly honoring a member—Catherine—who had not yet been canonized, it was Caffarini who convened a council to sing her praises. As a result, the Dominican order was given permission, in January 1413, to celebrate a feast day for Catherine—on April 30. Initially, her feast day was not included in the General Roman Calendar, which was not all that unusual. When it was finally added in 1597, it was marked on the day of her death, April 29. However, because this conflicted with the feast of St. Peter of Verona, Catherine's feast day was moved back again—in 1628—to April 30. In the 1969 revision of the Roman Catholic Calendar of saints, Catherine's feast day was restored to its traditional date of April 29, where it remains.

Getting even someone as memorable as Catherine recognized as a saint—called canonization—is a long and arduous process in the Catholic Church, but it is also a democratic one that starts with a grassroots conviction, one shared by many religious people,

that someone lived a very holy existence. From there, the proce-
dure unfolds in three phases. First, church officials conduct an
investigation into all aspects of the person's life, including their
writings, which are meticulously combed through for evidence
of virtuous actions. Once satisfied, the pope declares the person
"venerable." The next step, beatification, requires evidence of one
miracle that happened after the candidate's death. Finally, there
must be proof of yet more miracles after death—most likely two
or three in the 1400s—and only after this last step will the pope
canonize the saint. Usually the miracles involve the permanent
healing of someone—a healing that can't be explained by science.
To Catholics, this final miracle is God's stamp of approval, his
way of affirming the saint's presence with him in heaven.

The official process for declaring someone a saint can't even
begin until at least five years after the person's death. This waiting
period serves a valuable purpose by ensuring the endurance of the
person's reputation for holiness, as well as making certain the case
for sainthood can be evaluated objectively.

In Catherine's case, there was a span of more than 80 years
after her death before she was finally canonized by Pope Pius
II—also from Siena—in 1461. Centuries later, in April 1866,
another honor was bestowed when Pope Pius IX declared Catherine a co-patroness of Rome. In June 1939, Pope Pius XII named
Catherine, along with St. Francis of Assisi, a joint patron saint of
Italy. Then in 1970, in recognition of a holiness that is truly out-
standing, Pope Paul VI proclaimed Giacomo and Lapa Benincasa's child, never formally educated, a "Doctor of the Church,"
along with St. Teresa of Ávila. They were the first women to
receive this great honor. Reflecting on this truly incredible distinction, one scholar observed that Catherine "had a genius for
applying with a stunning common sense, to real individuals and

real life situations, the theological concepts she absorbed . . . She spoke and wrote out of who she was constantly becoming—as woman, friend, caregiver, thinker, mamma and teacher to her expanding famiglia, Dominican, and concerned member of a tormented church."

And the accolades didn't stop there. In October 1999, Pope John Paul II made her one of Europe's patron saints, along with Edith Stein and Bridget of Sweden, a nod to the role women have played in the ecclesial history of the continent. Catherine's also the patroness of the historically Catholic American women's fraternity, Theta Phi Alpha. One of Catherine's most famous sayings, "Nothing great is ever achieved without much enduring," is Theta Phi Alpha's motto. More recently, some Catholic Church experts have suggested Catherine be named the patron saint of the Internet because of her proclivity for letter writing. Indeed, she's often mentioned alongside the likes of St. Isidore of Seville, an educated scholar sometimes called "the schoolmaster of the Middle Ages" for his founding of schools devoted to all branches of learning.

Finally, I would be remiss to end this book without highlighting historian Gerald Parsons's exploration of the twists and turns of Catherine's cult status through the centuries. Indeed, his book *The Cult of Saint Catherine of Siena* is a fascinating look at how Catherine was held up as an agent of social and political unity for hundreds of years. Parsons said that as early as 1859 Catherine was promoted as an icon by those seeking to unify Italy—which had been divided into a number of competing states for more than 1,000 years—as a nation with no foreign rulers and constitutional rule. Nationalists viewed Catherine's causes—peace in Italy, a crusade against the infidels and the return of the pope to his rightful place in Rome—as aligned with their own goal of reconciling Italian Fascism with Italian Catholicism.

By the early twentieth century, Italian leaders were portraying Catherine as someone who would have supported the 1911 invasion of Libya, where Italy was engaged in a war against Turkey, and later Italy's activities in World War I. As Parsons notes, three days of prayer to Catherine were held in June 1915, a month after the Italian entry into the war. A few years on, in the 1920s, her so-called "Roman spirit" transformed her into something of a Fascist icon. In a 1929 article published by the International Center of Studies *Cateriniani*, she was linked with Benito Mussolini due to their shared commitment to the promotion of "the unity of the nation in the unity of faith." Mussolini, whose father had despised the church, also was no fan of religion, but he couldn't dismiss the benefits of currying favor with the Catholics. Therefore, he was all too willing to negotiate the mutually beneficial Concordat and Lateran treaties with the Vatican in 1929. The papacy recognized the state of Italy; the state of Italy recognized Catholicism as the state religion. Pope Pius XI hailed the deal as one that had "restored God to Italy and Italy to God." Meanwhile, Mussolini won the pope's assurance that priests and members of religious orders would abstain from actively dabbling in politics.

As the years went on, Catherine was painted with an even more blatantly pro-Fascist brush. She became a model for Fascist women and, in 1932, was named patron saint of the official Fascist girls' movement. In October 1935, Italy invaded Ethiopia as part of an imperial grab for Africa. Young members of the Fascist party raised money so that they could ship a painting of Catherine to Italian soldiers—for inspiration to keep them fighting.

When a marble bust of Catherine was unveiled in the Pincio Gardens in Rome, the accompanying speeches from Fascist politicians praised the "springtime of spiritual rebirth which shone with the actions of Italy's eminent *condottiero*, Benito Mussolini." They cited Catherine's push to return the papacy to Rome as proof that she believed the city should rule the world.

Catherine continued to be associated with Mussolini and three months before the start of World War II—on June 18, 1939—Catherine was declared by the government as the patron saint of the Fascist state. Six months later Mussolini—who as a young Socialist had railed against the church, going so far as to say that only idiots believe the Bible—vowed to support an extravagant renovation of the Sanctuary of St. Catherine in Siena. As soon as war broke out, Catherine was held up as Italy's protector—a spirit that could be called upon to make sure Italian soldiers were victorious. A booklet filled with Catherine's quotations was distributed among soldiers, published under three headings: Believe, Obey, Fight—Mussolini's motto. According to David Winner, author of the book *Al Dente: Madness, Beauty and the Food of Rome*, there's a particularly haunting image involving Catherine from World War II. It's a photo that shows the main square in Siena awash with flags, military uniforms and "Roman" salutes as the mummified head of St. Catherine is paraded around in a jeweled glass box to galvanize Italy's soldiers in their fight for Hitler on the Russian front.

After the war, Catherine's notoriety was appropriated yet again. As the protector of Italian soldiers, she was prayed to. Later, as the protector of Allied soldiers, she was prayed to again. When Italy embarked on postwar reconstruction, she was prayed to for encouragement. In the decades since, an appreciation for Catherine's example has grown. Today, Catherinian festivals around the world draw huge crowds. There's a St. Catherine of Siena Medical Center on Long Island, New York. There's a Catherine of Siena Virtual College in London.

What a journey this particular saint has traveled, with a reputation that developed first as an expression of Sienese civil pride, then as a focus for Italian civil pride and finally as an expression of European civil pride.

Catherine's influence rested in her absolute conviction that God's will and hers were aligned, and that she was the mouthpiece for her Savior. But in the end, one can also never forget that her story starts with a little girl raised during a time of war, chaos and spiritual agony. Even people who have never attended Mass can greatly appreciate the spunk of a girl who cut off her hair to protest being urged to marry and the confidence of a woman who spoke so bluntly to the most powerful of men.

I especially will forever admire that Catherine wasn't afraid to speak her mind. "You who were angels upon earth, have turned to the work of devils. You would lead us away from the evil that is in you, and seduce us into obedience to the Anti-Christ," she dared write to a group of cardinals. And she always thought of others and never of her own needs. "The poison of selfishness destroys the world," she once said. What a powerful sentiment then. What a powerful sentiment now.

Selected Bibliography

I've listed several books and articles that were used as sources but not the hundreds of other works, papers, letters, theses, articles and scientific journals that were also beneficial to me.

Becker, Marvin B. *Medieval Italy: Constraints and Creativity.* Bloomington: Indiana University Press, 1981.

Bell, Rudolph M. *Holy Anorexia.* Chicago: University of Chicago Press, 1985.

Brophy, Don. *Catherine of Siena: A Passionate Life.* New York: BlueBridge, 2010.

Bynum, Caroline Walker. *Holy Feast and Holy Fast: The Religious Significance of Food to Medieval Women.* Berkeley: University of California Press, 1987.

Cantor, Norman F. *The Civilization of the Middle Ages.* New York: HarperCollins, 1993.

Catherine of Siena. *Catherine of Siena: The Dialogue.* Edited and translated by Suzanne Noffke, O.P. New York: Paulist Press, 1980.

Dreyer, Elizabeth A. *Accidental Theologians: Four Women Who Shaped Christianity.* Cincinnati, OH: Franciscan Media, 2014.

Flinders, Carol Lee. *Enduring Grace: Living Portraits of Seven Women Mystics.* New York: HarperCollins, 1993.

Gardner, Edmund G. *Saint Catherine of Siena: A Study in the Religion, Literature, and the Fourteenth Century in Italy.* New York: Dutton, 1907.

Harrison, Ted. *Stigmata: A Medieval Mystery in a Modern Age.* New York: St. Martin's Press, 1994.

Hilkert, Mary Catherine. *Speaking with Authority: Catherine of Siena and the Voices of Women Today.* Rev. ed. New York: Paulist Press, 2008.

Kelly, John. *The Great Mortality: An Intimate History of the Black Death, the Most Devastating Plague of All Time.* New York: HarperCollins, 2005.

The Letters of Catherine of Siena. 4 vols. Edited and translated by Suzanne Noffke, O.P. Tempe: Arizona Center for Medieval and Renaissance Studies, 2000, 2001, 2007, 2009.

Luongo, F. Thomas. *The Saintly Politics of Catherine of Siena.* Ithaca, NY: Cornell University Press, 2006.

McDermott, Thomas, O.P. *Catherine of Siena: Spiritual Development in her Life and Teaching.* Mahwah, NJ: Paulist Press, 2008.

Murray, Paul, O.P. *The New Wine of Dominican Spirituality: A Drink Called Happiness.* London and New York: Burns & Oates, 2006.

O'Driscoll, Mary. *Catherine of Siena—Passion for the Truth, Compassion for Humanity: Selected Spiritual Writings.* New Rochelle, NY: New City Press, 1993.

Parsons, Gerald. *The Cult of St. Catherine of Siena.* Surrey, UK: Ashgate, 2008.

Pastor, Ludwig. *The History of the Popes from the Close of the Middle Ages.* Vol. I. 6th ed. Nendeln, Liechtenstein: Kraus-Thomson, 1969.

The Prayers of Catherine of Siena. Edited and translated by Suzanne Noffke, O.P. New York: Paulist Press, 1983.

Raymond of Capua. *The Life of Catherine of Siena.* Edited and translated by Conleth Kearns, O.P. Dublin & Wilmington: Dominican Publications and Michael Glazier, Inc., 1980.

Saunders, Frances Stonor. *The Devil's Broker: Seeking Gold, God, and Glory in 14th Century Italy.* New York: HarperCollins, 2004.

Saunders, Frances Stonor. *Hawkwood: Diabolical Englishman.* London: Faber and Faber, 2004.

Tuchman, Barbara W. *A Distant Mirror: The Calamitous 14th Century.* New York: Ballantine Books, 1978.

Tylus, Jane. *Reclaiming Catherine of Siena: Literacy, Literature, and the Signs of Others.* Chicago: University of Chicago Press, 2009.

Underhill, Evelyn. *Mysticism: A Study in the Nature and Development of Man's Spiritual Consciousness.* New York: E. P. Dutton, 1911.

Undset, Sigrid. *Catherine of Siena.* Translated by Kate Austin-Lund. New York: Sheed and Ward, 1954.

Winner, David. *Al Dente: Madness, Beauty and the Food of Rome.* New York: Simon & Schuster, 2013.

Index

Accidental Theologians (Dreyer), 141

Agnes (Catherine's aunt), 39

Agnes of Montepulciano, 24, 86–87

Al Dente: Madness, Beauty and the Food of Rome (Winner), 217

Al-Hakim bi-Amr Allah, 72
see also Crusades

Alighieri, Dante, 9, 13, 16

Anagni, Italy, 155, 163

Aquinas, Thomas
see St. Thomas Aquinas

Ashley, Benedict, 112

Augustine
see St. Augustine

Augustinian order, 77–78, 186

Avignon Captivity, 14

Avignon in Flower (Gail), 119–20

Barduccio di Piero Canigiani, 155, 191, 193, 196, 199–202

Bartolomeo (Catherine's brother), 8, 54, 64

Basilica of San Domenico, 6, 40, 206, 211

Basilica of Santa Maria in Trastevere, 166

Beaufort, Pierre Roger de, 64

Beauvoir, Simone de, 37

Benincasa family, 6, 9, 15, 17, 42, 64

Bergoglio, Jorge Mario
see Pope Francis

Biancina, Agnolino and Monna, 134, 136

Black Death, 1–6, 9, 11–12, 15, 55, 81–83, 86, 159, 210

Boccaccio, Giovanni, 4, 9

Book of Margery Kemp, 36

Butler, Josephine, 56

Byzantine Empire, 73

Caffarini, Tommaso, 44, 48, 50, 107, 109, 144–45, 200, 213

canonization, xviii, 25, 112, 164, 212–14

Castel Sant'Angelo, 180–81

Catherine of Siena
blood and, 105–20
correspondence, 175–91
early life, 1–17
Florence and, 157–60
Christianity and, 71–87
Crusades and, 75–76, 91, 97–98, 101–3, 106, 111, 113, 115, 124, 215
first vision of Christ, 19–34
illness and death, 193–207
legacy, 209–18
marriage to Christ, 35–51
move to Rome, 121–37
Pope Urban VI and, 160–73
public image, 53–69
wounds of Christ and, 89–103

writing of *The Dialogue*, 139–56
Charles of Durazzo, 185, 207
Church of St. Christina, 93, 128
Church of the Holy Sepulchre, 72–73
Church of the Saint, 205
Ciompi Revolt of 1378, 160–61
Colombini, Giovanni, 8
Colombini, Lisa, 8, 54, 133, 166, 206
Concordat treaty, 216
Constantine I (emperor), 73
Corneto, Italy, 128
Crusades
    battle cry of, 74
    Catherine of Siena and, 75–76, 91, 97–98, 101–3, 106, 111, 113, 115, 124, 215
    Duke of Anjou and, 124–25
    outbreak of, 73–74
    Pope Gregory XI and, 74–75, 98, 101, 115
    see also Holy Land
Cult of Saint Catherine of Siena, The (Parsons), 215

da Orvieto, Giovanni di Gano, 131
de Beaufort, Count Guillaume, 126
de Beaufort, Pierre Roger
    see Pope Gregory XI
de Cros, Jean (Cardinal), 152–53
de Giovanni Tegliacci, Niccolo, 31
de Luna, Pedro (Cardinal), 154
de Noellet, Guillaume (Cardinal), 98–99
della Fonte, Tommaso, 17, 133, 135, 144, 213
della Scala, Beatrice Regina, 102
di Benincasa, Giacomo (Catherine's father), 6–8, 15, 26, 31–34, 54–56, 64–66, 149, 214
di Bondone, Giotto, 198
di Clemente Gori, Francesca, 77
di Giovanni, Bona, 204

di Lando, Michele, 160
di Landoccio Pagliaresi, Neri, 77, 147–48, 189, 198, 201
di Piagente, Lapa di Puccio (Catherine's mother), 6–8, 17, 26–32, 40–42, 46–47, 55, 57, 65–66, 83, 91, 127–28, 133, 165, 201, 205–6, 212, 214
di Pipino, Francesco, 158, 166
di Ser Vanni, Nanni, 131
di Stefano, Giovanni, 206
di Toldo, Niccolo, 105–12, 134, 145
di Tozzo, Giovanni, 204
Dialogue, The (Catherine of Siena), 23, 33, 40, 139–46, 175, 178, 213
Divine Comedy (Dante), 13, 16
Dodici, 55, 64
Dominican order, 17, 31, 39–43, 48, 54, 78–80, 86, 90–91, 107, 136, 146, 164, 202, 206, 213, 215
Dominici, Bartolomeo, 90, 130, 144, 166, 199
d'Oristano, Mariano, 113
Dreyer, Elizabeth A., 141
du Puy, Gérard, 106, 115
Duke of Anjou, 124
D'Urso, Giacinto, 50

embargo on Florentine goods, 117, 155
Esperanza, Maria, 24–25
Ethiopia, 216
Ezekiel (prophet), 24

Fascism, 215–17
fasting, 46, 57, 59–61, 63, 95
Ferrer, Vincent, 164
Flete, William, 77–79, 130, 153, 186
Florence
    Catherine of Siena and, 61, 66, 79–80, 117–18, 135, 148–49, 155, 162, 190–91
    dialect, 9

Dominicans and, 79
education and, 17
papacy and, 90, 98–100, 102,
    114–18, 122–23, 125, 127,
    148, 151, 153, 161, 180, 185
plague and, 11
Siena and, 55, 91
social unrest, 155, 159–60
War of Eight Saints and, 90, 98
Franciscan order, 24, 39

Gail, Marzieh, 119
Giovanna (Catherine's sister), 7, 31,
    42
Graef, Hilda C., 23
Great Chapel and Library, 114
see also Palace of the Popes
Great Schism, 14, 154, 164, 167,
    176–78, 183, 186, 189, 206–7,
    210

Hawkwood, John, 75–76, 99, 150,
    181
Hildegard of Bingen, 140–41
Hilkert, Mary Catherine, 161
Hitler, Adolf, 217
Holy Land, xvii, 72–75, 102
see also Crusades
Holy Roman Empire, 131
Hundred Years' War, xvii
Hurtaud, Père, 146

indulgences, 201

Joan of Arc, 212

Karin (Bridget of Sweden's daughter),
    168–69
Kempe, Margery, 36
Kierkegaard, Søren, 24
King Charles V of France, 124, 154,
    170, 180, 183, 187
King David, 49
King Louis I of Hungary, 172, 185

King Philip IV of France, 12–13

Lapa
    see di Piagente, Lapa di Puccio
Lateran Palace, 167
Lateran treaty, 216
Levasti, Arrigo, 111
Libya, 216
Life of St. Catherine of Siena (Butler),
    56, 212
Livorno, Italy, 128
Lucca, Italy, 100–2, 114, 116
Luther, Martin, xiv, 12

Maconi, Stefano, 118–20, 128, 155,
    197
Mantellate, 39–42, 48, 65, 77, 118,
    165, 197
Margaret of Cortona
    see St. Margaret of Cortona
Mary Magdalene, 30, 68
Matteo di Ceni de Fazzio, 81
Middleton, Catherine (Kate), xviii
miracles, xiv, xvi, 60–61, 65, 86,
    94, 96–97, 135, 145–46, 189,
    203–5, 211–14
Miracoli of St. Catherine (Anonymous),
    64
Mussolini, Benito, 216–17
Myers, Rawley, 127
mysticism, xii, 23–25, 37, 50, 142

Naples, 97, 127, 152, 154, 164,
    168–69, 180, 182, 184–85,
    206–7
nationalism, 215
Noffke, Suzanne, xii, 47, 141, 154

O'Driscoll, Mary, 178
Orsini, Giacomo (Cardinal), 152–53
Ostia, Italy, 128, 170

Palace of the Popes, 14, 114
Palazzo della Signoria, 160

Palazzo Pubblico, 55–56
Parson, Gerald, 215–16
Perugia, Italy, 105–6, 185
Petrarch, Francesco, 9, 14
Pincio Gardens, 216
Pisa, Italy, 90–92, 96–97, 99, 101–2,
    105, 107, 113–17, 128, 171,
    202, 210
Pisano, Giovanni, 91
plague
    see Black Death
Pope Alexander V, 210
Pope Benedict XVI, xii, 54, 209, 211
Pope Boniface VIII, 12–13
Pope Clement V, 13
Pope Clement VI, 3, 13–14, 113
Pope Clement VII, 163–65, 168,
    172, 179–85, 187, 195, 207
Pope Francis, 209–11
Pope Gregory XI
    Agnani and, 155
    Bridget of Sweden and, 75, 89
    Catherine of Siena and, xvii,
        75, 89–90, 100–2, 120–23,
        135–36
    corruption in the Church and,
        98, 121
    Crusades and, 74–75
    death, 151, 154
    Duke of Anjou and, 124
    election, 64
    Florence and, 114–17, 123–25,
        149, 161
    Hawkwood and, 99
    Lucca and, 101
    Raymond of Capua and, 136, 148
    return to Rome, xvii, 126–30, 167
    selection of cardinals, 113–14
    Tuscany and, 98
    Urban VI and, 153, 171, 182
Pope John Paul II, xviii, 210, 215
Pope Leo XIII, 206
Pope Paul VI, 140, 214
Pope Pius II, xviii, 214

Pope Pius IX, 214
Pope Pius XI, 216
Pope Pius XII, 214
Pope Urban II, 73–74
Pope Urban V, 14, 63–64
Pope Urban VI
    Catherine of Siena and, 154–55,
        160–61, 165–66, 168–72, 176,
        184–87, 190, 194–96, 201,
        206–7
    Clement and, 164–65, 172,
        179–80
    dislike of, 154
    election, 153
    Florence and, 161
    Great Western Schism and, 164
    King Charles and, 187
    Naples and, 182, 207
    reforms and, 153–55
    vote for abdication of, 163–64
    war with Avignon forces, 179–84
Prayers of Catherine of Siena, The, 175
Prignano, Bartolomeo, 152–53
    see also Pope Urban VI
Prince William, xviii

Queen Giovanna of Naples, 97, 127,
    154, 168–70, 180–85, 207
Queen Mary of Hungary, 97

Raymond, Elias, 79
Raymond of Capua
    Avignon and, 117–18, 120
    Catherine of Siena and, 15–16,
        28–31, 33, 47, 54, 58–61,
        79–87, 89–93, 97, 107–8,
        112–13, 117, 122, 126, 130,
        132, 135–36, 139, 143–46,
        149–50, 157–58, 187–89,
        194–97, 200
    Catherine's death and, 202–7,
        212–13
    on Catherine's miracles, 61, 65
    on Catherine's visions, 21–23,

26–27, 39, 46, 49–50, 67,
111–12
Genoa and, 178
King Charles and, 187
Pope Gregory XI and, 148
Pope Urban VI and, 165, 169–72,
182
Reda, Mario, 59
Riformatori, 106, 134
riots, 55, 64–65, 127, 157–59
Robert of Geneva (Cardinal), 129,
168, 181
Rocca d'Orcia, 133–34, 145, 147,
155

Sabbatini, Giovanni, 54
Sacco, Giuseppe, 59
Salembier, Louis, 178
Salimbeni family, 55, 57, 132–36
Salutati, Coluccio, 100
Santa Maria church (Trastevere),
180, 182
Santa Maria della Scala hospital,
20, 64
Santa Maria sopra Minerva church,
136, 188, 202, 205
Saracini, Alessia, 60, 77, 166, 197,
206
Sarzana, Italy, 150–51, 155
Scivias (Hildegard of Bingen), 141
Scott, Karen, 146, 178
Second Sex, The (Beauvoir), 37
Sisters of Penitence, 41
Soderini, Niccolo, 80, 116, 155
spiritual espousal, 35
see also mysticism
St. Agnes, 169
St. Anthony, xxi, 26
St. Augustine, 78
St. Bernard of Clairvaux, xviii
St. Bridget of Sweden, xviii, 13, 64,
75, 89–90, 102, 168, 212, 215
St. Catherine of Alexandria, 35, 110
St. Catherine of Bologna, 205

St. Catherine of Sweden, 168
St. Dominic, 41, 49, 68, 206
see also Dominican order
St. Faustina Kowalska, 24
St. Francis of Assisi, 7, 24, 95–96,
210, 214
see also Franciscan order
St. Isidore of Seville, 215
St. John (apostle), 145
St. John the Evangelist, 21
St. Margaret of Cortona, 24, 63, 169
St. Paul, 21, 38, 95
St. Peter, 21
St. Peter of Verona, 213
St. Peter, tomb of, 167
St. Peter's Basilica, 128, 166–67,
180, 190, 198–99
St. Teresa Benedicta, xviii
St. Teresa of Ávila, 36–38, 140, 214
St. Thomas Aquinas, xv-xvi, 23, 78,
145
Stefani, Marchionne di Coppo
Stefano (Catherine's brother), 17, 20,
64, 66
Stein, Edith, xviii, 215
stigmata, 92–93, 95–96, 105, 196,
211
Story of a Soul (Thérèse of Lisieux),
141

Tantucci, Giovanni, 130, 144, 201,
203
Tebaldeschi, Francesco, 152–53
Tegliacci, Niccolo de Giovanni, 31
Teresa of Ávila
see St. Teresa of Ávila
Thérèse of Lisieux, 140–41
Theta Phi Alpha, 215
Turkey, 216
Tuscany, 1, 6, 8–10, 77, 89–90, 96,
98, 103, 150

Underhill, Evelyn, 25
Undset, Sigrid, 27, 147

Vadaterra, Alfonso da, 89–90
Val d'Orcia, 135
Vanni, Andrea, 40
Villani, Giovanni, 17
Virgin Mary
   Agnes of Montepulciano and, 86
   Basilica of Santa Maria, 166
   Catherine of Siena and, 27–29, 35,
      49, 61, 68, 83, 127, 197
   Feast of the Annunciation, xi
   Feast of the Purification of Mary,
      197
   St. Bridget of Sweden and, 64
   visions of, 24, 35, 61, 64, 68
Visconti, Bernabo, 102, 150
visions
   Catherine's spiritual awakening
      and, 25
   of Christ, xii-xiii, 21–23, 48–50,
      84–87, 111
   Ezekiel and, 24
   Margery Kempe and, 36
   of Rome, 189
   of speaking with God, 194–95
   St. Catherine of Alexandria and,
      35
   St. Francis of Assisi and, 96
   St. Teresa of Ávila and, 37
   Virgin Mary and, 61
   see also mysticism

War of Eight Saints, 90, 98, 180,
   185
Way of the Mystics, The (Graef),
White, Alfredo, xv, 25
Winner, David, 217
World War I, 216
World War II, 217